Criminal Justice in Britain

LONDON
HER MAJESTY'S STATIONERY OFFICE
1975

Prepared by
REFERENCE DIVISION
CENTRAL OFFICE OF INFORMATION, LONDON

346
CEN

93483

ISBN 0 11 700763 3

0108484

N.B. This pamphlet is one of a series produced by the Central Office of Information for British Information Services. To meet requests from inquirers in the United Kingdom, certain pamphlets in the series are being made available on sale from Her Majesty's Stationery Office.

CONTENTS

INTRODUCTION

THE UNDERLYING aim of criminal justice in the United Kingdom is to protect the community from disorder and anti-social behaviour while ensuring that offenders who break the law are detected and dealt with according to well-defined legal principles. Broadly speaking, four fairly distinct stages are involved: the enactment of criminal legislation which, for example, defines prohibited acts, establishes criminal courts and provides for the treatment of offenders; the prevention of crime and the enforcement of the law—largely matters for the police service; the determination by the courts of the guilt or innocence of offenders, and the selection of appropriate sentences for the guilty; and the treatment of convicted offenders, both within the community and within custodial establishments.

The criminal law deals with wrongful acts harmful to the community at large and punishable by the State. Like most other forms of law in the United Kingdom, it largely derives from 'common law' (the ancient law of the land, as deduced from custom and interpreted in court cases by the judges) and 'legislation' (laws made by, or under the authority of, Parliament). In the event of conflict, legislation takes precedence over the common law. (European Community law, a third source of United Kingdom law generally, is mainly confined in impact to economic affairs.)

Although the United Kingdom is a unitary state, it does not have a single body of law or a single penal system universally applicable within its limits. England and Wales on the one hand and Scotland on the other have their own distinctive legal systems, law courts and, to a lesser extent, penal procedures. Substantial similarity exists on many points, but considerable differences remain in organisation and practice. In Northern Ireland the system of criminal justice has traditionally resembled that in England and Wales, although the recent political instability and violence have necessitated the introduction of special temporary measures. This pamphlet deals primarily with England and Wales, but reference is made to Scotland and Northern Ireland where there are substantial points of difference in practice and procedure.

The law undergoes constant reform in the courts as established principles are interpreted, clarified or refashioned to meet new circumstances. Substantial changes in the law, however, are the responsibility of Parliament through the normal legislative process.[1] Proposals can be introduced either by the Government of the day or by an individual member of Parliament, although in practice most public legislation is Government-sponsored. The Government departments usually concerned with criminal justice matters are the Home Office, the Lord Chancellor's Office, the Law Officers' Department, the Scottish Home and Health Department, the Lord Advocate's Department and the Northern Ireland Office. Their specific responsibilities are outlined elsewhere in this pamphlet. There is normally considerable consultation between the Government departments concerned and, for example, professional bodies, voluntary organisations and other agencies interested in

---

[1]Described in COI reference pamphlet, *The British Parliament*, R5448.

1

the subject-matter of proposals for new legislation. On criminal justice matters the Government might consult, as necessary, representative organisations of the legal profession, the police, the courts, the prison service and the probation and after-care service, and such voluntary groups as the Howard League for Penal Reform, Justice (the British section of the International Commission of Jurists), the National Association for the Care and Resettlement of Offenders and the National Council for Civil Liberties. Legislation sponsored through Parliament by a private member of Parliament, rather than by a Government minister, may have Government support (the Rehabilitation of Offenders Act 1974, see p 5, is a recent example), and may be in part the result of a campaign for change carried out by a pressure group.

Two statutory Law Commissions (one for England and Wales and one for Scotland), the Criminal Law Revision Committee, the Advisory Council on the Penal System (in England and Wales), the Scottish Council on Crime and various special committees of inquiry (appointed as needed) are among the official bodies which advise on aspects of criminal justice.

Crime prevention and crime investigation, the preservation of the peace and the arrest and bringing to trial of offenders are primarily the concern of the police service, although it has been recognised since the days of the earliest police forces that public approval and co-operation are essential to the maintenance of law and order. Police work inevitably includes a broad range of 'social' functions—ranging from special juvenile liaison and community relations schemes to involvement, for instance, with family problems and health matters. Policemen, like all citizens, are subject to the rule of law, and are legally responsible for their actions in carrying out their duties.[1]

One of the most important aspects of British criminal justice is the independence of the judiciary, which is free to administer the law under the protection of the law without fear or favour. It is well established that the executive may not disturb or delay the course of justice.

A safeguard against corruption or prejudice in the administration of the criminal law is provided by the jury system which, since the twelfth century, has involved ordinary, independent citizens as an integral part of all important criminal trials.

It is a fundamental principle that proceedings in court should be held in public. There is, therefore, a right of access by the public to every court, other than in special circumstances such as cases involving children (where the child's right of privacy is considered paramount) or matters of State security. Court proceedings are reported in the press, and, when a trial has finished (but not before), comments may also be published, provided that they are not calculated to bring a court or a judge into contempt, or to interfere with the course of justice.

Criminal law in the United Kingdom presumes an accused person to be innocent until he has been proven guilty beyond resaonable doubt, and every possible step is taken to deny the prosecution any advantage over the defence. An accused person cannot be compelled to give evidence at his

---

[1] COI reference paper, *Human Rights in the United Kingdom*, R5625, illustrates from British law and practice how the United Kingdom has pursued and implemented the aims and principles of the United Nations Universal Declaration of Human Rights.

trial; if he remains silent, the prosecution is not allowed to comment on the fact (the judge, however, may do so if he thinks fit). Witnesses normally give evidence in person in open court—the use of written evidence is much less common than, for instance, in the courts of most other Western European countries. A distinctive feature of criminal trials in the United Kingdom is the 'adversary procedure' under which the court reaches a decision on the basis of legal arguments advanced and the facts alleged and proved by prosecution and defence lawyers, who conduct the examination of witnesses. Again, this contrasts with the 'inquisitorial procedure' common in the rest of Western Europe, under which the judge conducts his own legal research and personally examines witnesses.

Every accused person has the right to employ a legal adviser for his defence and, if he cannot afford to pay his legal costs, he may be granted legal aid at public expense. If he is remanded in custody, he may be visited in prison by his legal adviser so that his case may be properly prepared. An accused person found guilty of any crime usually has a right of appeal to a higher court.

Courts of law are responsible for deciding what sentence an offender should be given. Except for treason and piracy with violence (which still carry the death penalty), they can impose no punishment of greater severity than imprisonment.

The sentencing of offenders is increasingly based on the idea that measures for social rehabilitation are more effective in reducing crime (as well as more desirable from an ethical point of view) than punitive measures alone. Growing emphasis is placed on treatment within the community rather than within a custodial establishment. When determining sentences, courts have a number of options, and, as far as possible, try to select the type of punishment most appropriate for the individual offender concerned. Special provisions cover the treatment of children and young people under the age of 17 who commit offences, and of young offenders aged 17 to 20 years. Britain abides by the standard minimum Rules for the Treatment of Offenders, adopted by the United Nations in 1955. The main agencies concerned with the treatment of offenders are the probation and after-care service (in Scotland local authority social work departments) and the prison service.

THE CRIMINAL LAW

A FEATURE common to each of the domestic legal systems of England and Wales, Scotland and Northern Ireland is the distinction made between criminal law and civil law. The distinction lies less in the nature of the acts and omissions covered by the two categories than in the subsequent legal proceedings and the hierarchy of law courts involved. The same wrongful act may often be both a crime and a civil wrong (for example, reckless or dangerous driving, a criminal offence, may also give rise to a civil action if it results in injury to, or damage to the property of, other people); and there is as a rule no reason why a criminal prosecution and a civil action should not both be brought, since proceedings are quite separate and independent, and take place before different courts. Broadly speaking, however, whereas civil law relates to the rights, duties and obligations of individuals between themselves,[1] criminal law is concerned with wrongs affecting the community at large—acts contrary to the order, peace and well-being of society which render the offender liable to punishment by the State.

In most cases the criminal law recognises a particular intention or state of mind as a necessary ingredient of a criminal offence (there are some cases of 'strict liability'). Ignorance of the law on the part of an accused person is, however, never accepted as an excuse. The law punishes not only criminal acts but also—as incitements, attempts or conspiracies—steps towards the commission of a crime which may never take place. A person may be exempted from criminal liability because he has been deprived of his free will and self-control—by coercion or insanity, for instance. Some classes of people, such as children under 10 years and overseas diplomats, may also be exempted from liability.

The classification of crimes may be based on the kind of harm done. There are crimes, for instance, against the person of the individual (such as assault or murder), against his or her property (burglary, arson and theft are examples) and against public rights which belong in common to all citizens (such as treason and offences against public order). Classification may also be based on the methods of 'trial' (as criminal proceedings are known); serious crimes are usually tried 'upon indictment' before a judge and jury, while the less grave are tried 'summarily' before magistrates sitting without a jury.

The Prerogative of Mercy

The administration of justice is one of the prerogative powers of the Crown, but has long been exercised only through the judiciary and the courts (nowadays the courts are almost entirely founded on a statutory basis). Offences against the law are breaches of the Queen's peace and, because the courts dispense the Queen's justice, the right to pardon such offences is vested in the Crown. The prerogative of mercy is an exceptional remedy

---

[1]Civil law, with which this pamphlet is not concerned, includes for instance family law, the law of property, the law of contract and the law of torts (notably, negligence, trespass and defamation). COI reference pamphlet, *The English Legal System*, R5312, provides an outline of both civil law and criminal law procedures in England and Wales.

which may be used where justice or humanity calls for some interference with the strict course of the law. It may be invoked to right a wrongful conviction which cannot otherwise be corrected, or to mitigate sentence. Exercised on the advice of the Home Secretary, the Secretary of State for Scotland or the Secretary of State for Northern Ireland, the prerogative may take the form of the grant of a free pardon, a conditional pardon substituting one form of punishment for another, or a remission reducing a sentence or penalty without changing its character.

Rehabilitation of Offenders

Under the Rehabilitation of Offenders Act 1974 a person convicted of an offence who subsequently remains free of a further conviction for a specified number of years—the 'rehabilitation period'—is not in most circumstances obliged to disclose the fact of his or her original conviction. He or she then becomes a 'rehabilitated person', and the conviction is treated as 'spent'.

The rehabilitation period is calculated on the basis of the sentence imposed for the original conviction, but sentences of more than two and a half years' imprisonment are outside the scope of the Act. The longest rehabilitation period laid down by the Act, ten years, applies to sentences of between six and 30 months' imprisonment. The shortest is six months—in the case of an offender receiving an absolute discharge (see p 33). The rehabilitation period can be prolonged if, during it, further offences are committed.

In general, the Act operates by making evidence of spent convictions inadmissible in civil (though not criminal) courts and in proceedings before a wide variety of other tribunals and disciplinary bodies. A 'rehabilitated person' is also entitled to deny the existence of his or her spent convictions in reply to questions asked out of court—for instance, when applying for employment. The law of defamation is amended so that in proceedings brought by a rehabilitated person over the publication of his or her spent conviction, the defendant may not rely on a defence of 'justification' in England and Wales or of 'veritas' in Scotland if it can be proved that the publication was made with malice. The Act also creates a criminal offence of disclosure of official records relating to spent convictions otherwise than in the course of official duty.

The Home Secretary or the Secretary of State for Scotland have power in a number of circumstances to vary the Act's application by means of statutory instruments subject to affirmative resolution in Parliament. They may for example specify circumstances in which a full and truthful answer may be required of a rehabilitated person to a question about his or her previous convictions— this might be necessary when certain kinds of employment are involved. Details of the orders to be made under the Act have not yet been worked out.

Criminal Injuries Compensation Scheme

The Criminal Injuries Compensation Scheme was established in 1964 to provide *ex gratia* compensation to victims of crimes of violence and people hurt as a result of attempts to arrest offenders and prevent offences. The scheme is administered by the Criminal Injuries Compensation Board, which comprises legally qualified members appointed by the Home Secretary and the Secretary of State for Scotland after consultation with the Lord

Chancellor. Compensation, which is assessed on the basis of common law damages and takes the form of a lump-sum payment, amounted to over £4 million in 1973–74, and has totalled over £19 million since the scheme began. A review of the scheme is in progress with a view to putting it on a statutory basis.

The scheme does not apply in Northern Ireland where there is statutory provision in certain circumstances for compensation from public funds for both criminal injuries and malicious damage to property.

Criminal Statistics

The differences in the legal systems of the constituent countries make it impracticable to analyse in detail trends in crime for the United Kingdom as a whole, but some overall figures may be given. In 1973 over 1·5 million serious crimes and offences were recorded as known to the police. The total number of people proceeded against for all types of offences was more than two million: a fifth for the more serious offences, and well over half for motoring offences. The number of people found guilty of non-indictable and miscellaneous offences has grown less rapidly than the number found guilty of the more serious types of offence.

In England and Wales most of the indictable offences known to the police (80 per cent in 1973) comprise burglary, theft and unauthorised taking or the handling of stolen goods. In the majority of the burglaries, thefts and unauthorised takings (excluding cars and pedal cycles) the value of property stolen or taken is less than £10 and in only a comparatively small proportion is it over £100.

The numbers of indictable offences known to the police in England and Wales in 1973, and the numbers cleared up, are indicated in Table 1.

The rate of increase of the number of known offences involving violence against a person has been more rapid than that for other offences (the increase between 1972 and 1973 was 17 per cent), but in 1973 the total formed

Table 1

OFFENCES RECORDED AS KNOWN TO THE POLICE AND CLEARED UP: ENGLAND AND WALES 1973

Offence group	Number of offences known to the police	Offences cleared up	
		No.	%
Violence against the person ..	61,299	50,165	81·8
Sexual offences	25,736	19,953	77·5
Burglary	393,165	146,971	37·4
Robbery	7,338	3,374	46·0
Theft and handling stolen goods	698,798	235,138	33·6
Fraud and forgery	110,673	91,219	82·4
Criminal damage	52,815	20,459	38·7
Other offences	7,833	7,303	93·2
TOTAL	1,357,657	574,582	42·3

Soucre: *Criminal Statistics 1973.*

less than 5 per cent of all known indictable offences in England and Wales. Within the group, most offences are assaults. Sexual offences formed almost 2 per cent of the total of known indictable offences—a proportion which has remained fairly constant over the past few years.

Known offences involving firearms in England and Wales during 1973 totalled some 4,670. They included not only 2,480 in which a firearm was used (that is, fired, used to threaten or used as a blunt instrument) or carried for possible use (101), but also offences in which a firearm was stolen, handled or obtained by fraud or forgery (2,089). Of the offences in which a firearm was used, two-thirds involved an air weapon and half of the remainder involved a long-barrelled or sawn-off shotgun. An appendix to this pamphlet (p 53) contains a note on United Kingdom regulations to control firearms.

The 'clear-up' rate[1] for known indictable offences was 42·3 per cent in

Table 2

PEOPLE FOUND GUILTY BY OFFENCE GROUP:
ENGLAND AND WALES 1973

Offence group	People found guilty	
	No.	%
Indictable offences		
Theft and handling stolen goods	180,875	9·4
Burglary	54,362	2·8
Criminal damage	33,223	1·7
Violence against the person	33,041	1·7
Fraud and forgery	16,105	0·8
Sexual offences	7,169	0·4
Robbery	3,159	0·2
Other indictable offences	9,512	0·5
Non-indictable offences		
Motoring offences	1,191,808	61·8
Intoxicating liquor law	105,200	5·4
Revenue law	92,997	4·8
Wireless telegraphy offences	42,734	2·2
Highway Act offences	22,551	1·2
Social security, etc, offences	12,881	0·7
Assault	12,054	0·6
Drug offences	11,988	0·6
Railway offences	11,417	0·6
Disorderly behaviour	8,851	0·5
Other non-indictable offences	78,741	4·1
TOTAL	1,928,668	100·0

Source: *Criminal Statistics 1973.*

[1]Including offences for which a person is arrested or summoned, or for which he is cautioned; those attributed to children under the age of criminal responsibility; those taken into consideration by a court when an offender is found guilty on another charge; and certain of those of which a person is known or suspected to be guilty but for which he cannot for some reason be prosecuted (for example, because he has died).

1973 (the 1972 figure was 41·1 per cent). This overall rate conceals regional variations (the rate for England and Wales outside the London area was 46·9) and wide variations for different types of offence: 82 per cent of known offences of violence were cleared up, for example, compared with 30 per cent of known thefts.

Of the people found guilty of all types of offence in 1973, some 337,000 (17·5 per cent) were guilty of indictable offences, see Table 2.

Just under half those found guilty of indictable offences in England and Wales in 1973 were aged under 21 years. Of all persons found guilty, comparatively few, about 13 per cent, were women. More than three-quarters of the women offenders were found guilty of theft or handling, whereas only about half the men were found guilty of these offences.

The number of people found guilty of offences or formally cautioned by the police for offences other than non-indictable motoring offences is indicated in Table 3.

Local chief officers of police in England, Wales and Scotland have a statutory duty to supply either the Home Secretary or the Secretary of State for Scotland with statistics relating to offences, offenders, criminal proceedings and the state of crime in their areas. Abstracts of this information are published each year by the Home Office and the Scottish Office as *Criminal Statistics (England and Wales)* and *Criminal Statistics (Scotland)*. Further information about crime trends (as well as about the police service) is

Table 3

PEOPLE FOUND GUILTY AND PEOPLE CAUTIONED, BY AGE, SEX AND TYPE OF OFFENCE: ENGLAND AND WALES 1973

Age and sex	Indictable offences		Non-indictable offences		
			Non-motoring offences		Motoring offences
	Found guilty	Cautioned	Found guilty	Cautioned	Found guilty
MALES					
Under 14 ..	19,855	34,510	2,300	2,559	783
14–16 ..	52,067	25,728	16,397	6,370	16,900
17–20 ..	75,874	3,901	49,922	2,206	123,647
21 and over	144,491	5,189	287,634	14,681	967,843
All ages ..	292,287	69,328	356,253	25,816	1,109,173
FEMALES					
Under 14 ..	1,949	9,762	152	246	20
14–16 ..	5,267	7,331	1,748	742	341
17–20 ..	8,392	595	4,740	1,748	5,040
21 and over	29,551	3,775	36,521	4,555	77,234
All ages ..	45,159	21,463	43,161	7,291	82,635
ALL PERSONS ..	337,446	90,791	399,414	33,107	1,191,808

Source: *Criminal Statistics 1973.*

contained in the annual reports of Her Majesty's Inspector of Constabulary, Her Majesty's Chief Inspector of Constabulary for Scotland and the Commissioner of Police of the Metropolis. Special statistical reports, *Offences Relating to Motor Vehicles* and *Offences of Drunkenness*, are published each year in England and Wales. The annual *Report on the Administration of Home Office Services in Northern Ireland* contains both criminal and civil judicial statistics. Research studies concerned mainly with criminal statistics are prepared periodically by the Home Office Statistical Department.

Criminological Research and Studies

A wide range of criminological and other social research is carried out by the Home Office Research Unit which also provides liaison on research matters between the Home Office and the Social Work Services Group of the Scottish Home and Health Department. Research is also carried out in university departments and by various other research organisations, much of it financed by the Home Office and the Scottish Home and Health Department. Studies undertaken in the Home Office Research Unit are mainly concentrated on subjects of direct interest to the home departments. The results of the unit's work are published in learned journals and, in the Home Office Research Studies series, by Her Majesty's Stationery Office.

Among studies by the unit is a series of projects being carried out in five probation and after-care areas to evaluate the provision of more intensive and matched treatment for high risk offenders (see p 38). Other studies include research on criminal histories and reconvictions in order to provide a basis for measuring the relative effectiveness of various types of treatment for various classes of offender, to help to determine the kind of prisoner for whom provisions such as pre-release hostels and parole are necessary and effective. The results of non-custodial measures are also being examined. In the field of community action and the prevention of crime, studies are being carried out to describe and measure the incidence of vandalism.

The principal university research establishment in the field, the Institute of Criminology at Cambridge, in addition to conducting research on its own account, provides a postgraduate course in criminology. The research projects at Cambridge include a study of criminal victimisation, perceptions of crime and attitudes to criminal justice, a comparative study of known criminal violence, and the sentencing policy of the Court of Appeal (Criminal Division).

First degree courses (normally in law, sociology or social administration) which include some study of criminology are available at the following universities: Aberdeen, Bath, Birmingham, Edinburgh, Exeter, Keele, Leeds, London, Manchester, Newcastle upon Tyne, Nottingham, Oxford, Reading, Sheffield, Southampton and Warwick. One-year postgraduate courses are held at the universities of Cambridge, Edinburgh, Hull, Keele, London (the London School of Economics and Political Science and University College) and Sheffield. Research facilities exist at the universities of Bath, Birmingham, Edinburgh, Hull, Oxford, Sheffield and Southampton. Research supported by Home Office grants is being carried out by the universities of Bristol, Cardiff, Hull, London and Oxford. The Scottish Home and Health Department is supporting research by the universities of Aberdeen, Edinburgh,

Glasgow and Stirling. The research topics covered include a review of Part 1 of the Children and Young Persons Act 1969, the definition and explanation of crime, an evaluation of a prison for long-term offenders, and juvenile delinquency.

Law Reform

The duty of keeping the law under review in order to ensure that it meets the needs of modern society lies with the Law Commission (for England and Wales), the Scottish Law Commission, the Criminal Law Revision Committee and the Law Reform Committee (which does not deal with criminal law).

The Law Commissions are permanent bodies comprising lawyers of high standing appointed by the Lord Chancellor or the Secretary of State for Scotland and the Lord Advocate. They are charged with the duty of scrutinising the law with a view to its systematic development and reform.

The commissions submit programmes of reform to the Government, and may recommend further examination of specified topics by themselves or some other body. Their work can embrace all aspects of the law; in the field of criminal law, for instance, the commission for England and Wales is working towards codification.

The Criminal Law Revision Committee, a standing body of judges and lawyers appointed by the Home Secretary, examines aspects of English criminal law referred to it by him.

Many professional bodies and other organisations and individuals also publish papers, books and pamphlets from time to time advocating change in some or other aspect of the law.

Public Expenditure

Table 4 indicates the level of public expenditure in the United Kingdom on justice and law in 1951–52, 1961–62 and in the five financial years between 1969 and 1974.

Table 4

PUBLIC EXPENDITURE ON JUSTICE AND LAW: UNITED KINGDOM
£ million

	1951–52	1961–62	1969–70	1970–71	1971–72	1972–73	1973–74
Police	73	156	342	411	474	506	588
Prisons	7	23	56	64	84	98	119
Legal aid	—	4	15	19	23	29	38
Probation and after-care	8	23	11	14	17	22	26
Parliaments and Law Courts			49	59	69	85	103
Total	88	206	473	567	667	740	874
of which: Capital expenditure	8	16	40	43	53	52	93

Source: *Social Trends 1974.*

THE POLICE SERVICE

THE POLICE service in England, Wales and Scotland is organised in a number of large forces linked with local government and subject to the influence and eventual control of the Home Secretary (in England and Wales) and the Secretary of State for Scotland. In Northern Ireland, it is organised in a single force.

Forces

There are 43 regular police forces in England and Wales, and 20 in Scotland. Each is responsible for a separate area, but there is constant co-operation between them. They are defined according to their areas of responsibility. Outside London most counties have their own forces, though in the interests of efficiency several have combined forces; in London the Metropolitan Police Force is responsible for an area within a radius of about 15 miles (24 kilometres) from the centre, but excluding the City of London where there is a separate force. From May 1975 in Scotland the 20 existing forces will be replaced by six regional and two combined forces.

The strength of the regular police force in England, Wales and Scotland is over 111,000 (including nearly 5,000 policewomen), the size of individual police forces depending on the area and population which they serve. In England and Wales, outside Greater London, strengths of individual forces vary considerably, the average being about 2,350 officers. The strength of the Metropolitan Police Force is about 21,000. In Scotland forces' strengths range from about 115 to 2,850.

In addition to the regular police forces, there are constabularies maintained by the statutory transport and other public authorities, and by the Ministry of Defence.

Considerable numbers of people are employed by commercial security organisations. Subject to the ordinary law of the land, the companies' work involves, for example, the protection of cash in transit, the carriage of important documents, advice on all aspects of security and the safeguarding of trade secrets.

Police Authorities and Chief Constables

Each of the regular police forces is maintained by a police authority. In England and Wales the authority is a committee consisting of local councillors and magistrates. Combined police authorities, which also comprise councillors and magistrates, contain representatives from each constituent county.

The police authority for the Metropolitan Police Force is the Home Secretary. In the City of London the Court of Common Council is the police authority, although it usually appoints a standing committee to deal with all police matters on its behalf.

From May 1975 in Scotland the police authority will be the regional or island council (a joint police committee where there are combined forces).

The primary duty of the police authority is to provide an adequate and efficient police force for the area for which it is responsible. Its powers, some of which are subject to ministerial approval, include the appointment of the chief constable and deputy and assistant chief constables of the force and, if necessary, calling upon them to retire; fixing the establishment of the force and the number of officers in each rank; appointing traffic wardens; and providing and maintaining buildings and premises as well as vehicles, apparatus, clothing and other equipment required for police purposes.

In the Metropolitan Police area the chief officer of police and his immediate subordinates are appointed by the Crown on the recommendation of the Home Secretary.

Chief constables are responsible for the direction and control of police forces and for the appointment, promotion and discipline of all ranks below deputy or assistant chief constable; they are, however, generally answerable to the police authorities on matters of efficiency, and are required to submit a written annual report.

Northern Ireland

The Royal Ulster Constabulary (RUC) operates under the direction of a chief constable who is responsible to the Police Authority for Northern Ireland, which has a duty to maintain an adequate and efficient police service. The RUC has a strength of almost 4,500. Ranks, conditions of service, pay and general duties follow closely on the lines of the service in the rest of the United Kingdom. The RUC is aided in its duties by the civilian Royal Ulster Constabulary Reserve, a largely part-time body of men and women; while on duty they have the same powers, privileges and duties as members of the regular force.

Central Authorities

The Home Secretary and the Secretary of State for Scotland, who have a general responsibility for the preservation of law and order throughout England, Wales and Scotland, are concerned both in the overall organisation of the police service and in its administration and operation. They approve the appointment of chief constables, and may require a police authority to retire a chief constable in the interests of efficiency, call for a report from a chief constable on any matters relating to the policing of his area, or cause a local inquiry to be held. They are also empowered to make regulations, with which all police authorities must comply, covering such matters as rank; qualifications for appointment, promotions and retirement; discipline; hours of duty, leave, pay and allowances; and uniform and equipment. Some of these regulations are first negotiable in the Police Council (on which are represented the police authorities, police staff associations and ministers); the others are discussed on representative advisory bodies together with any general questions affecting the police.

Inspectors of Constabulary

All police forces in England, Wales and Scotland (except the Metropolitan Police for which the Home Secretary is directly responsible) are subject to inspection on behalf of the Secretaries of State. Inspectors of constabulary carry out, under Her Majesty's Chief Inspector of Constabulary and Her Majesty's Chief Inspector of Constabulary for Scotland, a formal annual inspection of the forces in their regions, inquiring into efficiency and reporting to the Home Secretary or the Secretary of State for Scotland. Annual reports are published, covering the whole range of police matters. The inspectors also maintain close touch on all matters with the forces for which they are responsible, and have various advisory functions.

Finance

The income of police authorities derives from central Government, the 'rates' (a form of local property tax) and various other local sources. The Government's contribution, which (except in the case of the City of London Police, where it is a third) is a half of approved expenditure, is conditional on the Home Secretary or the Secretary of State for Scotland being satisfied that the force is being efficiently administered and maintained.

Officers and Ancillary Staff

The standard police ranks in England, Scotland and Wales are: chief constable, assistant chief constable, chief superintendent, superintendent, chief inspector, inspector, sergeant and constable.

The chief officer of the Metropolitan Police, the Commissioner of Police of the Metropolis, is assisted by a deputy commissioner and four assistant commissioners. Next in rank are deputy assistant commissioners, and then commanders; from chief superintendent the ranks are the same as in the rest of the country. In the City of London the ranks are the same as in the regions except that the chief officer is the Commissioner of Police and the second in command is an assistant commissioner.

Police Cadets

Cadet training is designed to prepare boys and girls between 16 and 18½ years of age[1] for a career in the police service. They have no police powers, but in addition to their educational studies and physical training they are given instruction in elementary police work.

Civilian Staff

In order to release as many uniformed police officers as possible for operational duties, police authorities employ about 30,000 civilians on administrative (pay, records, finance, and other general subjects) and other duties (fingerprint, scenes of crime and control room work). Some are also employed on catering and domestic duties.

Traffic Wardens

Traffic wardens (of whom there are about 7,000) are extensively employed to discharge specified duties connected with road traffic and vehicles, normally undertaken by the police. In this connection they may be authorised to serve fixed penalty notices[2] for minor offences to which the fixed penalty system applies; to man police car-pounds (except in Scotland); to enforce the

---

[1]There are a few forces which do not recruit girls.

[2]A fixed penalty notice gives the recipient the option of paying a specified sum to the clerk of the appropriate court instead of having his case tried in the ordinary way.

vehicle excise laws; and to obtain the names and addresses of people thought to have committed certain types of traffic offences. They may also be employed to direct traffic, to act as parking attendants at street parking places, and as school-crossing patrols, if the police agree. Traffic wardens remain under the control of the chief constable of the force to which they are attached, whatever duties they may perform.

Special Constables

Each police force has an attachment of special constables, who are volunteers willing to perform police duties without pay in their spare time. In England and Wales the function of special constables is to act as auxiliaries to the regular force when required. In Scotland they are employed only in emergencies although they may be assigned to duty for training purposes.

Duties

A police officer in the United Kingdom is an independent holder of public office and exercises powers as a constable, whether conferred by statute or by common law, by virtue of his office. He is an agent of the law of the land, not of the police authority nor of the central Government and, although his chief officer of police has a vicarious liability for any wrongful act he may commit in the performance of his functions as a constable, he himself may also be sued in respect of his own wrongful act.

No member of the police service may belong to a trade union since it is a basic principle of the service that its members must not only be free from political bias, but must also be seen to be free from it. All ranks, however, have their own associations which can make representations to ministers or to police authorities on matters of interest or concern to their members.

The many and varied functions of a police officer as a constable range from the protection of people and property, road or street patrolling and traffic control to crime prevention, criminal investigation and the apprehension of offenders. In urban areas particularly, where the heart of many police problems lies, policemen are increasingly called upon to deal with social difficulties, with responsibility to bring in other social agencies and expert help when needed. The police in England and Wales also have the tasks of examining evidence and approving charges, and must often decide whether or not to grant bail (see p 19).

Police Departments

The main departments in all police forces are the uniform department, the criminal investigation department and the traffic department. Many forces also have specialised departments, river or marine police (in areas with long stretches of navigable waterway or coastline), a mounted branch and dog handlers.

The bulk of police work devolves upon members of the uniform department, who are generally responsible for the preservation of the peace, the prevention of crime, the protection of people and property and the maintenance of law and order. In most urban areas these duties are carried out under a system known as 'unit beat policing' which, by combining foot patrols using personal radio sets with police cars, provides great flexibility of manpower deployment, and makes full use of modern communications techniques. The functions of the uniform department also include the inspection of places of public entertainment and the investigation of reports of lost property. Most police forces have formed 'task forces'—mobile groups of a dozen or more uniformed officers—whose functions include attending serious emergencies, organising widespread searches, providing protection against outbreaks of vandalism and patrolling areas where burglaries are prevalent. The groups are formed from patrol constables who are attached for short spells and then resume their normal duties.

Criminal investigation departments, in addition to investigating crime, deal with the checking and classification of crime reports, with the collection of all kinds of information relating to crime in the district, with the preparation of crime statistics and with crime prevention measures.

Traffic departments, as well as enforcing road traffic laws, are concerned with traffic management, road safety and related matters. Traffic patrols also perform any other police work which they may find necessary in the course of their patrols.

Since the Metropolitan Police fraud squad was established in 1946, special police departments have been formed in London to deal, for instance, with stolen vehicles, bank robberies, arts and antiques, obscene publications, drugs, serious crimes and bombings. The same trend towards training detectives for specialised duties has been followed elsewhere in the country—for example, to deal with drugs or fraud cases. A Central Drugs Intelligence Unit at Scotland Yard, staffed by Home Office, customs and police experts, collects, evaluates and disseminates information on dangerous drugs matters to enforcement agencies throughout the country. On the security side, the 'Special Branch' protects the safety of prominent people and is concerned with individuals or groups who may be engaged in espionage or other subversive activities.

Policewomen often specialise in matters involving women and children, and much of their work takes them to juvenile courts and welfare institutions. They nevertheless have the same powers, pay and conditions of service as men, work for both the uniformed and detective branches, and can be called upon to help in any kind of investigation, working as a team with their male colleagues.

Crime Prevention

The prevention of crime, primarily a police service function, is organised in two principal ways: through the work of a special department in each force, and through the duties of the policeman on patrol (officers are encouraged, for example, to look for circumstances offering opportunities to criminals—such as buildings which are not properly secured). The size of crime prevention departments varies from force to force, but functions are similar and include: the study of methods used by criminals and of ways of combating them; advising on ways of carrying cash and valuables, protecting buildings against intruders, preventing fraud, securing vehicles and their contents, and using safes and strongrooms; the co-ordination of prevention work among all ranks in the force; the training of personnel; and the organisation of exhibitions, lectures and publicity campaigns. Permanent crime prevention exhibitions are displayed at most local police head-quarters. Frequent campaigns on aspects of crime prevention are promoted nationally by the Home Office and the Scottish Home and Health Department using, for instance, television, the press and leaflets delivered to every home.

The Home Office Standing Committee on Crime Prevention brings together representatives of commerce and industry on the one hand and police officers and Home Office officials on the other. In the larger towns crime prevention panels enable prominent citizens—in commerce, industry, the press and local voluntary organisations—to help the police in the fight against crime.

Co-ordination between Forces

A number of common services are provided by the central Government departments for the benefit of all forces to supplement those provided by the police authorities for their own use and by communal arrangements made between the forces themselves. The most important of these services are: training services; a forensic science service in England and Wales which provides eight regional laboratories (in addition to the Metropolitan Police Laboratory); telecommunications services, including depots, which in England and Wales supply and maintain wireless equipment for the police; and central and provincial criminal records which are available to all forces. In addition, regional crime squads, consisting of teams of experienced detectives from several forces, operating under a committee of chief constables, are employed in England and Wales to investigate major crimes involving inquiries in more than one police area. The Scottish Crime Squad assists police forces in Scotland in the investigation and prevention of crime and in the collection and maintenance of information concerning criminals. Arrangements are also made for everyday assistance by one force to another.

Scientific Planning and Research

There are three interrelated branches of the Home Office Police Department devoted to scientific research and medium- and long-term planning. The Police Scientific Development Branch and the Police Research Services Branch, which are staffed by senior police officers, are concerned with operational research into police methods and the development of equipment for police forces throughout England, Wales and Scotland. The Police Management and Planning group, which is composed mainly of economists and accountants, is responsible for the development of a planning-programming-budgeting system for the police, and for the medium- and long-term planning of police resources.

In all aspects of police work, the application of scientific aids has reached an advanced stage: about £20 million is spent annually on police equipment, including about £3 million on radio communications. The police have some 30,000 personal radio sets operational. A police national computer is being developed for rationalising the keeping of records[1] and speeding up the dissemination of information.

---

[1] Police records are confidential; they may only be disclosed to third parties within very strict limits laid down by the central Government.

Metropolitan Police Force Services

Services provided by the Metropolitan Police Force for other forces include (1) the publication of the *Police Gazette*,[1] which contains particulars of people wanted for crime and details of stolen property, and is supplied to the police forces of the United Kingdom and to certain other Commonwealth and foreign forces; (2) the organisation and control of the Special Branch of the criminal investigation department at New Scotland Yard, whose duties include the protection of royalty, some ministers and distinguished foreign visitors; and (3) the carrying out of extradition orders made by the courts. The Metropolitan Police Force is also available, on request, to assist any other police force in England and Wales in criminal investigations. Similarly, the services of the Fraud Squad, run jointly by the Metropolitan Police Force and the City of London Police, are available throughout England, Wales and Scotland for the investigation of serious company frauds. The National Central Bureau, which handles the business of the International Criminal Police Organisation (Interpol) on behalf of the United Kingdom and the British dependencies, is part of the Metropolitan Police Force. For certain of these services, the Metropolitan Police Force receives an additional Exchequer grant.

Relations with the Public

Because of the small number of police officers in relation to the population as a whole (roughly one officer to 500 people), the limitations on their powers and their lack of firearms, the sanction of the police in enforcing laws rests to a very considerable extent upon common consent—the basic concept of the service is that its members serve the public that they represent and receive assistance from the public they serve.

Police training courses place increasing emphasis on the role of both the service and the individual officer in local communities. All forces are concerned with schemes for dealing with problems before court action becomes necessary, particular attention being paid to relations with children and young people and with coloured immigrant communities.[2]

In London and other large cities, for example, juvenile bureau schemes provide a service for dealing with children and young people arrested on minor charges. The schemes, which involve parents, schools and the probation service as well as the police, often result in the administering of a caution in cases where it is not considered necessary or desirable to take a child to court.

Considerable use is made of radio and television programmes and documentary films involving members of the public in police problems and putting the police point of view; plays and dramatised series also present aspects of police work.

Complaints against the Police

In England and Wales every chief officer of police is required to record and investigate any complaint received from the public about a member of his force. He may, if it seems advisable, request the chief officer of another

---

[1] The Scottish Criminal Record Office in Glasgow is responsible for the publication of the *Scottish Police Gazette*.
[2] For further information see COI reference pamphlet, *Race Relations in Britain*, R5934.

force to provide the investigator (and must do so if the Home Secretary so directs). Moreover, unless he is completely satisfied that no criminal offence has been committed, he must send the papers to the Director of Public Prosecutions (see p 28), with whom rests the decision as to whether or not criminal proceedings should follow. If a complaint results in a disciplinary hearing, the complainant is entitled to attend as an observer. Government proposals to introduce an independent element into the handling of complaints would involve the establishment of an independent statutory commission with members drawn from national or regional panels and with a full-time staff. The commission would consider complaints in the light of an initial police investigation and before any decision had been taken on whether or not disciplinary proceedings should be brought.

The penalties which may be imposed following a disciplinary hearing are: caution, reprimand, fine, reduction in rank, requirement to resign and dismissal from the force. An officer who has been dealt with for a disciplinary offence can appeal to the Home Secretary (or the Secretary of State for Scotland) against finding or punishment, or both.

In Scotland, too, chief constables have a duty to arrange for the investigation of complaints; procurators fiscal investigate independently complaints alleging that an officer has committed a criminal offence.

Police authorities and all inspectors of constabulary throughout England, Wales and Scotland must keep themselves informed about the way in which chief officers handle complaints.

Powers

The powers of the police are complex and governed by statutes, cases decided by the courts and administrative practices. This section, which deals in the main with the position in England and Wales, is only intended to indicate very roughly the nature and extent of some of their more important aspects.

A police officer who exceeds his authority unlawfully or unnecessarily is subject to disciplinary procedure, and possibly to civil or criminal proceedings. Conversely, it is an offence for any member of the public to obstruct, or attempt to obstruct, an officer in the execution of his duty, or to refuse to assist an officer in making an arrest when called upon to do so in a case of reasonable necessity. Members of the public are also expected to give all possible help to a police officer in tracking down and apprehending a criminal, and to report any crime or suspicious behaviour they may witness.

Police officers are not generally armed, but in an emergency firearms can be issued on the authority of a senior officer to suitably trained men. On normal patrol duties a police officer carries a wooden truncheon, which he may use only in self-defence or to restore order when all other means have failed.

Arrest

A citizen's basic right to move about freely is protected by law; physical restraint can only be justified on certain grounds. There is no general power of arrest, nor have the police any general powers to detain suspects or witnesses.

Under English law arrest may be effected either on a warrant issued by a judicial authority on sworn information laid before it, or in certain cases without a warrant under powers conferred by statute or common law. (Private citizens, as well as police officers, have certain powers of arrest.) Arrest involves an element of compulsion, but no more physical force must be used than is reasonably required. On being arrested without a warrant, a person must be informed of the grounds on which he is being detained unless the circumstances of the arrest prevent this. Arrest warrants must specify the name of the person to be arrested and details of the offence. A general warrant to search for and arrest an unnamed person is illegal. Warrants are issued only where the nature of the alleged offence justifies arrest; in other circumstances a summons to appear in court is usually issued—if the person summoned does not appear, a warrant for his arrest can then be issued.[1]

Bail

A person who has been arrested without a warrant must either be brought before a magistrates' court within 24 hours (excluding Sundays) or, if this is not practicable, be released on bail unless the offence appears to a senior police officer to be a serious one. Where the arrest is made under a warrant, the warrant is usually either backed for bail, in which case the person must be released as soon as the necessary 'recognisances' (see below) have been found, or it requires the person to be brought before a magistrates' court at once. Magistrates' powers to refuse bail[2] are generally restricted to cases where the defendant is accused of a serious offence or is likely to commit further offences or to abscond, or where remand in custody is necessary for the defendant's protection. When bail is granted, broadly speaking the person arrested must 'enter into a recognisance' whereby he undertakes to forfeit a sum of money unless he appears at the date of the next hearing; he may also be required to find other people to act as 'sureties' for his appearance. Application can be made to the Crown Court or the High Court against refusal of bail or against the conditions on which it is offered.

---

[1] The Prevention of Terrorism (Temporary Provisions) Act 1974, which embodies a programme of security measures designed to help to eradicate terrorism in connection with Northern Ireland affairs, contains provisions which affect, among other things, powers of arrest and search. The Act which became operative in November 1974 is to remain in force for six months and will then expire unless renewed by affirmative parliamentary approval of a ministerial order.

The Act provides the police with powers to arrest a person whom they reasonably suspect of being concerned in the commission, preparation or instigation of acts of terrorism, or is subject to an exclusion order under the Act, and to detain him on their own authority for 48 hours—a period which may be extended by the Home Secretary for up to seven days.

The Home Secretary is empowered under the Act to make an order providing for the examination of travellers entering or leaving England, Wales, Scotland or Northern Ireland. Examining officers may be police or immigration officers or officers of customs and excise, and their powers may extend to searching people under examination and to arresting and detaining them if necessary.

[2] Some changes in the bail system in England and Wales were recommended by a Home Office working party which reported in May 1974: *Bail Procedures in Magistrates' Courts*, HMSO, 73p, ISBN 0 11 340560 X. In some areas defendants on remand who are suitable for bail but have no fixed place of abode can be sent (as a condition of bail) to a bail hostel. An experimental hostel has existed in London since 1971, and the experiment is being extended to other areas by probation committees and voluntary bodies.

Entry, Search and Seizure

Any person—police officer or private citizen—has the right to enter premises in a reasonable manner to save life or to prevent serious injury to people or property, but there is no general right of entry, search or seizure of property without the consent of the individual concerned or lawful authority —under common law (for example, to prevent a breach of the peace), statute, warrant issued by a judicial authority or, in a few special cases, the written permission of a senior police officer.[1] Police officers are not allowed in the absence of specific authority to search a person before arrest in the hope of finding evidence to support charges. A few statutes (some of them of local extent only) entitle a police officer, for example, to stop people suspected of possessing property or drugs unlawfully. After an arrest a prisoner may be searched where his behaviour makes it prudent to search him for his own protection or that of the police. He may also be searched if it is likely that he possesses, for example, stolen goods, housebreaking tools or other articles which may be useful as evidence. The seizure of articles not material to any criminal charge is not legally justified, and all articles must normally be returned once legal proceedings are over unless a court orders otherwise. Female prisoners are searched by women police officers.

Questioning

The procedure to be followed in the questioning of people who may subsequently be put on trial is governed partly by a set of rules laid down by judges and partly by rules of evidence (highly technical rules of law concerned with the proof of facts); confessions of guilt are inadmissible during a criminal trial if procured by duress or material inducements; and an accused person does not have to give evidence at his trial.

The Judges' Rules[2] are for the guidance of the police and do not have the force of law, but statements obtained contrary to them may be rejected by the trial judge. The rules are designed to ensure that questioning is not oppressive; that statements to the police are voluntary; and that a person is notified, by formal cautions, that he is not obliged to say anything in answer to questions, first when the police have reasonable grounds for suspecting him of being guilty of an offence, and again when they charge him or tell him that he may be prosecuted. Once a person has been charged with an offence the police may not ask any further questions other than to prevent or minimise harm or to clear up an ambiguity in a previous answer or statement. At every stage of a police investigation a suspect must be allowed access to legal advice provided that this is unlikely to impede the processes of investigation or the administration of justice.

Identification

When a person is charged with an offence, his fingerprints can be taken with his consent. If the consent is not given, a senior police officer may apply to a magistrates' court for an order authorising the taking of fingerprints (if

---

[1]In addition modern statutes give certain powers of entry, for example, to inspectors of food and drugs, public health inspectors and inspectors of the gas and electricity boards.

[2]*Judges' Rules and Administrative Directions to the Police*, HMSO, 1964, 14p, ISBN 0 11 340419 0.

needed, reasonable force may then be used to take them). If the prisoner has not previously been convicted and is later acquitted or the case is dropped, all copies of fingerprints taken under such an order must be destroyed. There are regional fingerprint bureaux in England and Wales, as well as the fingerprint branch of the Metropolitan Police.

Strict rules also govern the use of other methods of identification, such as identification parades. A committee of inquiry is examining all aspects of the law and procedure relating to evidence of identification in criminal cases.

Unlawful Detention

A person detained in custody who thinks that the grounds for his detention are not lawful,[1] may seek a writ of *habeas corpus* against the person who detained him, this person then being required to appear before the court on the day named to justify the detention. An application for such a writ is normally made to a divisional court of the High Court either by the person detained or by someone acting on his behalf. If no court is sitting the application may be made to a single judge who may, and in some cases must, direct that it should come before a divisional court. An application on behalf of anyone under 18 years is always first made to a judge sitting in chambers or in private. A writ may be refused only by a divisional court.

Scotland

In Scotland the police have very broadly the same powers of arrest as have the police in England and Wales. The Judges' Rules do not apply, but when anyone is arrested he must be cautioned and have the charge read over to him. Thereafter, only his voluntary statements can be used in evidence at his trial, and the court will reject any statements made by him unless it is satisfied that they have been fairly obtained. As in England and Wales, when anyone is apprehended in Scotland he must be brought before the court competent to deal with his case with the least possible delay. Where a prosecution on indictment is contemplated, the accused is brought before a judge for judicial examination and the judge may then commit him for trial or for further examination. Eight days may elapse between commitment for further examination and commitment for trial.

People in custody in Scotland, other than those charged with murder or treason, may be liberated on bail by the sheriff or, if the offence is within the jurisdiction of a summary court other than the sheriff court, by that court or by the police. Even in the case of murder or treason, bail may be granted at the discretion of the Lord Advocate or the High Court of Justiciary. There is a right of appeal to the High Court by the accused person against the refusal of bail, by the prosecutor against the granting of bail, or by either party against the amount fixed. The writ of *habeas corpus* does not apply in Scotland, but the High Court of Justiciary has power to release anyone unlawfully detained, and trials must, in any event, be brought to a conclusion within 110 days of committal to custody.

---

[1]Lawful grounds are: in pursuance of criminal justice; for contempt of court or of either House of Parliament; detention of persons found to be mentally disordered; detention of children by their parents or guardians; and detention expressly authorised by Act of Parliament.

CRIMINAL COURTS

Courts in England and Wales[1]

Magistrates' courts deal with about 98 per cent of all persons convicted of criminal offences in England and Wales, and conduct preliminary investigations into the more serious offences. The Crown Court takes all criminal work above the level of magistrates' courts. An official committee is reviewing the distribution of business between the two types of court.

Magistrates' Courts

There are some 900 magistrates' courts throughout England and Wales, served by 21,500 lay magistrates ('justices of the peace'), 49 stipendiary magistrates (who are full-time salaried lawyers) and over 400 legally qualified justices' clerks. The chief work of the courts is the hearing and determination of charges against people accused of summary offences—that is to say those offences that may legally be disposed of by magistrates sitting without a jury. The release of defendants on bail pending trial is a function of both the police and magistrates' courts (see p 19).

Magistrates may try certain serious offences which would otherwise be tried on indictment provided that the defendant has been given the opportunity to elect to be tried by jury, and told that, if he consents to summary trial, he might, upon conviction, be sent to a higher court for sentence. Magistrates also sit as 'examining justices' to conduct preliminary inquiries to determine whether there is sufficient evidence to justify the committal of the accused for trial in the Crown Court; evidence given at these proceedings cannot be reported at the time except at the defendant's request, unless the magistrates discharge him. On conviction magistrates cannot, as a rule, impose a sentence of more than six months or a fine exceeding £400. They may, however, commit an offender for sentence at the Crown Court if his offence carries a higher penalty and if, after obtaining information about his character and antecedents, they consider their sentencing power inadequate. They may also bind an offender over by requiring him to enter into recognisances, with or without sureties, to be of good behaviour or to keep the peace, discharge him absolutely or conditionally, or put him on probation.

Magistrates' courts normally consist of a bench of three lay magistrates whose function is to ascertain the facts and apply the law to them with the help and advice of a clerk of the court who is both legal adviser to the magistrates and in charge of the administrative functions of the court.

In some large provincial cities, where the pressure of work is heavy and continuous, there are also stipendiary magistrates, who usually sit alone. In inner London, there is a unified system of courts in which either a metropolitan stipendiary magistrate or lay magistrates may sit; and in the City of London, the aldermen of the City are magistrates by virtue of charters, in addition to the magistrates appointed individually.

To hear cases involving young people under 17 years of age brought before the court in care or criminal proceedings the courts sit as *juvenile courts* (see p 46).

---

[1]For further information see COI reference pamphlet, *The English Legal System*, R5312.

The Crown Court

The Crown Court is served by High Court judges and Circuit judges and by Recorders who sit on a part-time basis. It sits regularly at nearly 90 centres.

The criminal law jurisdiction of the Crown Court comprises trials on indictment (broadly, for the more serious offences), the sentencing of those committed for sentence from magistrates' courts and appeals from magistrates' courts.

A High Court judge, Circuit judge or Recorder presides at all trials of the Crown Court with a jury. A Circuit judge or Recorder sits with between two and four magistrates for appeals and committals for sentence from magistrates' courts, and may sit with magistrates for the less important trials on indictment. For the more important criminal trials, a High Court judge sits without any magistrates. In the City of London, where the Crown Court is known as the Central Criminal Court, the Lord Mayor and aldermen are entitled to sit with any High Court judge, Circuit judge or Recorder in any class of work. The distribution of Crown Court business is determined by directions given by, or on behalf of, the Lord Chief Justice of England, with the concurrence of the Lord Chancellor; such directions allocate the various classes of offences to High Court judges, Circuit judges and Recorders.

Appeals

A person convicted by a magistrates' court may appeal against the conviction or against the sentence to the Crown Court. Where the appeal is on a point of law either the prosecutor or the defendant may appeal from the magistrates' court to the High Court by way of case stated—that is, by requesting the magistrate to 'state a case for the opinion of the High Court'. In certain cases, an appeal by case stated may lie to the High Court from the Crown Court, but normally appeals from the Crown Court, either against conviction or against sentence, are made to the Court of Appeal (Criminal Division). Appeals against conviction may be brought to the court by right on any point of law, and with leave of the trial judge or the court on any question of fact or mixed fact and law. Appeals against sentence come with the leave of the court, provided that the sentence was in the discretion of the trial judge and not fixed by law. The Court of Appeal (Criminal Division) normally consists of three judges, who may be Lords Justices of Appeal or judges of the High Court, although the Lord Chief Justice or a Lord Justice of Appeal usually presides. A further appeal from the Court of Appeal (Criminal Division) to the House of Lords can be brought if the court certifies that a point of law of general public importance is involved and it appears to the court or the House of Lords that the point is one that ought to be considered by the House. In addition, a prosecutor or defendant may appeal to the House of Lords from a decision of the Divisional Court in a criminal case.

The Attorney General (see p 26) may seek the opinion of the Court of Appeal on a point of law which has arisen in a case where a person tried on indictment is acquitted; the court has power to refer the point to the House of Lords if necessary. The acquittal in the original case is not affected, nor is the identity of the acquitted person revealed without his consent.

Courts in Scotland

Criminal cases in Scotland are heard either under solemn procedure, when proceedings are taken on indictment and the judge sits with a jury, or under summary procedure, when the judge sits without a jury. All cases in the High Court of Justiciary and the more serious ones in the sheriff court are tried under solemn procedure. Proceedings are taken under summary procedure in the less serious cases in the sheriff court, and in the lay summary courts.

Lay Summary Courts

The District Courts (Scotland) Bill at present before Parliament provides for a new system of district lay summary courts to replace the existing burgh and justice of the peace courts when Scottish local government is reorganised on 16 May 1975.[1]

Sheriff Courts

Sheriff courts (which also exercise extensive civil jurisdiction) have both solemn and summary procedure, although most prosecutions are brought as summary complaints. The sheriff—the judge of the court—can impose up to two years' imprisonment in cases on indictment and three months' imprisonment in summary cases. He can remit cases deserving more serious penalties to the High Court for sentence.

The High Court of Justiciary

The High Court of Justiciary is Scotland's supreme criminal court. It is both a trial court and an appeal court. Any one of the following judges is entitled to try cases in the court: the Lord Justice General (who is also the Lord President of the Court of Session), the Lord Justice Clerk, or any one of 18 Lords Commissioners of Justiciary. The seat of the court is in Edinburgh, but the judges go on circuit to preside at trials in other towns.

Appeals

A person convicted in the High Court or in a sheriff court on indictment may appeal to the High Court of Justiciary (a) against his conviction on any ground which involves a question of law alone, or, with leave of the High Court or upon the certificate of the judge who presided at the trial that it is a fit case for appeal, on any ground, and (b) against his sentence, with the leave of the High Court, unless the sentence is one fixed by law. Appeals are heard by three or more judges, and there is no further appeal to the House of Lords.

A person convicted summarily may appeal to the High Court, but only on questions of law and procedure, and not on issues of fact.

Courts in Northern Ireland

The superior courts in Northern Ireland comprise the Supreme Court of Justice and the Court of Criminal Appeal, both of which sit in Belfast. The High Court is the superior court of first instance, and comprises the Lord

---

[1]See COI reference pamphlet, *Local Government in Britain*, R5505.

Chief Justice and five judges. The Court of Criminal Appeal, which is the appellate tribunal in criminal cases tried on indictment, consists of the Lord Chief Justice and all the judges of the Supreme Court, but sittings normally comprise two or three judges. Appeals to the House of Lords from the Court of Criminal Appeal lie under similar conditions as from the English Court of Appeal (Criminal Division).

The inferior criminal courts are the county courts and courts of summary jurisdiction, 'petty sessions'. The county courts are presided over by judges, of whom there are ten, who sit with a jury to try cases of the more serious sort on indictment. The county court judge sits alone to hear appeals from the magistrates' courts. Magistrates' courts are presided over by a resident magistrate who sits alone, and corresponds to a stipendiary magistrate in England and Wales. Juvenile courts are similar to those in England and Wales. As a temporary arrangement in Northern Ireland certain offences involving violence or explosives may be tried by a High Court or county court judge sitting alone.

Coroners' Courts

Coroners' courts are common law courts convened when a person appears to have died a violent or unnatural death or a sudden death of which the cause is unknown, and in certain other circumstances. Cases may be brought to the notice of the local coroner (a senior lawyer or doctor) by doctors, the police, various public authorities or members of the public, and it is his duty to hold an inquiry into how, when and where the deceased died. He may hold an inquest in court, and must do so if he has reason to believe that the deceased has died a violent or unnatural death or has died in prison or in circumstances for which legislation provides that an inquest must be held. If the coroner has reason to suspect murder, suicide, manslaughter or infanticide, or that the death was caused in a road accident, he must summon a jury.

The office of coroner does not exist in Scotland: the procurator fiscal inquires privately into all sudden and suspicious deaths in his district, and reports on his inquiries to the Crown Agent in order that Crown counsel may consider what proceedings, if any, are required.

Administration of the Courts

In the United Kingdom the judiciary is independent of the executive and is therefore not subject to ministerial direction or control in regard to the judgment of the courts. Responsibility for administrative matters in England and Wales, when it does not rest with the courts themselves, lies partly with the Lord Chancellor and partly with the Home Secretary; in Scotland and Northern Ireland it lies with the appropriate Secretary of State. In England and Wales the Lord Chancellor is concerned with the composition of all criminal courts and with parts of criminal procedure, and the Home Secretary with criminal law, preventing offences, apprehending offenders, part of the process of trying them, and virtually the whole of their treatment. The Prime Minister is concerned in that he is responsible for recommending to the Crown the highest judicial appointments. The Secretary of State for the Environment is responsible for providing accommodation for all the superior courts, except the Central Criminal Court in London which is the special responsibility of the City of London.

The Lord Chancellor is the senior member of the judiciary of England, Wales and Northern Ireland. He sits from time to time as the presiding judge in the Judicial Committee of the House of Lords which hears appeals to the House. He is also a senior member of the Government, and is the Cabinet minister responsible for the administration of justice and the running of all courts, save magistrates' courts (which are the responsibility of the Home Secretary). He is responsible for the appointment of judges and magistrates and of officers of the civil and higher criminal courts of law.

Magistrates' courts are mainly administered by magistrates themselves, chiefly through local committees, but the elected local authorities, with financial assistance from the Government, are responsible for meeting their costs, and the Home Secretary, besides exercising a general oversight, has certain specific responsibilities, including the approval of boundary changes, approval of the appointment of justices' clerks, and deciding disputes on financial matters.

In Scotland the Secretary of State appoints the staff of the High Court of Justiciary, and is responsible for the composition, staffing and general organisation of the sheriff courts.

In Northern Ireland members of the judiciary are appointed by the Lord Chancellor. The Northern Ireland Office is responsible for the staffing and general organisation of the county and petty sessions courts.

Law Officers of the Crown

The Attorney General and the Solicitor General—known as the Law Officers of the Crown for England and Wales—are the Government's principal legal advisers, and represent the Crown in appropriate domestic and international cases. Appointed from among senior counsel, they are members of the House of Commons, hold ministerial posts and change with the Government. The equivalent Scottish officers are the Lord Advocate and the Solicitor General for Scotland. Besides exercising a variety of civil law functions, the Attorney General has the ultimate responsibility for the enforcement of the criminal law in England and Wales, and the Director of Public Prosecutions (see p 28) is subject to his superintendence. The Attorney General is concerned with the institution and prosecution of certain types of criminal proceedings (see p 28). In carrying out these powers, he must, by convention, exercise an independent discretion, and must not be influenced by his Government colleagues (though he may consult them). The Solicitor General is subject to the authority of the Attorney General, with similar rights and duties.

The Law Officers of the Crown in Scotland are the Lord Advocate and the Solicitor General. They are the chief legal advisers to the Government on Scottish questions and the principal representatives of the Crown for the purposes of litigation in Scotland. The Lord Advocate is closely concerned with questions of legal policy and administration. Since private prosecutions are now virtually unknown in Scotland, the Lord Advocate is responsible for the public prosecution of all crimes. (At present, he does not control the prosecution of minor crimes coming before the lay summary courts, but the situation is under review because of the impending reorganisation of these courts—see p 24). He delegates most of the work of prosecution to the Solicitor General, to seven advocates-depute (who are collectively known as 'Crown Counsel') and to procurators fiscal (who are full-time legally qualified prosecutors). Although procurators fiscal are subject to the direct control of the Lord Advocate, they are primarily responsible for the prosecution of crimes in the sheriff court. They are also required to investigate all serious criminal offences which they then report to Crown counsel for the latter's instructions. The permanent adviser to the Lord Advocate is the Crown Agent who is also the head of the Procurator Fiscal Service. The Crown Agent is assisted by a staff of civil servants known collectively as the Crown Office.

The Judiciary

The courts of the United Kingdom are the Queen's Courts (since the Crown is the historic source of all judicial power), and the Sovereign, acting on the advice of ministers, is responsible for all appointments to the judiciary. In England and Wales appointments to the highest positions are made on the recommendation of the Prime Minister, while the Lord Chancellor recommends the appointment of High Court judges, Circuit judges and Recorders and the metropolitan and other stipendiary magistrates. Lay magistrates are appointed on behalf of the Crown by the Lord Chancellor,[1] who is advised by local advisory committees.

In Scotland the Prime Minister makes recommendations for the appointment of the most senior judges. Recommendations for the appointment of all other judges lie with the Secretary of State for Scotland. He is responsible for the appointment and removal of justices of the peace. In Northern Ireland county court judges and resident magistrates are appointed by the Crown on the advice of the Lord Chancellor. Lay magistrates are appointed by the Lord Chancellor.

Full-time judges do not engage in politics, except that the Lord Chancellor, as well as being head of the judiciary and Speaker of the House of Lords, is a leading member of the Government in power. With the exception of lay magistrates, judges are normally appointed from practising barristers, advocates or solicitors, and neither their training nor their career is in any way dictated by the State. Lay magistrates need no legal qualifications, being appointed for their qualities of integrity and understanding and as broadly representative of the community which they serve. On appointment, however, they give an undertaking to complete a period of basic training, so that they may obtain a sufficient knowledge of the law, including the rules of evidence, and may understand the nature and purpose of sentencing. Magistrates' work is unpaid, although there are allowances for travelling, subsistence and loss of income incurred in attendance at court.

In certain circumstances (for instance, in cases of misconduct or proven incapacity) judges of the inferior criminal courts in England, Wales and Northern Ireland may be removed from their position by the Lord Chancellor, and in Scotland, subject to specified conditions, by an order made by the Secretary of State on a report prepared by the Lord President of the Court of

---

[1]Except in Lancashire, where the Chancellor of the Duchy of Lancaster acts on behalf of the Crown in this matter.

Session and the Lord Justice Clerk. This latter order is subject to annulment by resolution of either House of Parliament. In order to safeguard and perpetuate the independence of the judiciary from the executive, however, superior judges in England, Wales and Northern Ireland (other than the Lord Chancellor who, as a Cabinet minister, changes with the Government) are subject to a power of removal only by the Sovereign on an address presented by both Houses of Parliament. In Scotland there is no statutory provision for removal of judges of the High Court of Justiciary from office and it is probable that special legislation would be required to effect such a dismissal.

Prosecutions

Prosecution is a discretionary matter which in practice normally rests, in England, Wales and Northern Ireland, with the police and, in Scotland, with public prosecutors. Police outside Scotland have powers, especially in the case of young people, to issue cautions instead of prosecuting.

All criminal trials in the United Kingdom are accusatorial—that is to say, they take the form of a 'contest' between the Crown and the accused person. In most cases in England and Wales a private individual may institute criminal proceedings, but in practice they are usually initiated and conducted by the police.

Some offences, however, can only be prosecuted by or with the consent of the Attorney General or the Director of Public Prosecutions. Where the consent of the Attorney General is required—for example, under the official secrets legislation—such prosecutions are invariably in the hands of the director.

The director, a senior civil servant and prominent lawyer, appointed by the Home Secretary but responsible to the Attorney General, has the duty of prosecuting all serious offences, which must be reported to him by the police. In addition, he gives advice to the police and others concerned with the administration of the criminal law, and has the power, where necessary, to take over criminal proceedings instituted by another prosecutor.

The director has other miscellaneous functions—for example, in connection with complaints of criminal offences by policemen, extradition and offences committed by foreign servicemen stationed in England and Wales.

Professional officers of the director's department are either barristers or solicitors, and, although the former have a right of audience in the higher courts, they do not in practice appear other than in magistrates' courts where they and their solicitor colleagues conduct summary and committal proceedings. When cases go for trial, counsel in private practice are instructed to appear on the director's behalf; at the Central Criminal Court in London these are drawn from a panel of 'Treasury Counsel' appointed by the Attorney General.

Each year the director's department conducts between 5 and 10 per cent of the prosecutions brought on indictment in England and Wales; it also conducts some summary prosecutions. In 1973 over 3,000 prosecutions were completed by the director.

The Director of Public Prosecutions in Northern Ireland is responsible to the Attorney General, who is also the Attorney General for Northern

Ireland. The director has functions which include the initiation of criminal proceedings in certain circumstances, representing the Crown in criminal actions, and prosecuting offences against statutory provisions on behalf of Government departments.

The prosecution process in Scotland is quite different from that in the rest of the United Kingdom. Through the Crown Office the Lord Advocate and subordinate prosecutors are responsible for the prosecution of practically all crimes before Scottish courts (except the lay summary courts which have their own public prosecutors). The Crown Office is concerned with the preparation of prosecutions in the High Court; the public prosecutors in the sheriff courts are known as 'procurators fiscal', and are lawyers who are usually full-time civil servants. The police make preliminary investigations of all offences known to them, and report the details to the procurator fiscal, who has a discretion whether or not to prosecute, subject to the discretion and control of the Crown Office. Private prosecutions, though permitted in some circumstances, are very rare in Scotland.

Trial

Since criminal law in the United Kingdom presumes the innocence of an accused person until his guilt has been proved, the prosecution is not granted any advantage, apparent or real, over the defence. A defendant has the right to employ a legal adviser for his defence, and if he cannot afford to pay he may be granted legal aid wholly or partly at the public expense (see p 31); if remanded in custody he may be visited in prison by his legal adviser to ensure that his defence is properly prepared. During the preparation of the case, it is customary for the prosecution to inform the defence of any relevant documents which it is not proposed to put in evidence, and to disclose them if asked to do so. The prosecution must inform the defence of any witnesses whose evidence may assist the accused and whom the prosecution does not propose to call.

Criminal trials in England and Wales are (with rare exceptions) held in open court, and the rules of evidence (which are concerned with the proof of facts) are rigorously applied. For instance, although generally the evidence of one uncorroborated witness is, as a matter of English law, sufficient, where the evidence is that of an accomplice (or accomplices) the judge will warn the jury of the danger of convicting on such uncorroborated evidence, and a conviction made without any such warning would not be upheld on appeal.

During the trial the defendant has the right to hear and subsequently to cross-examine (normally through his lawyer) all the witnesses for the prosecution; to call his own witnesses who, if they will not attend the trial of their own free will, may be legally compelled to attend; and to address the court either in person or through his lawyer—the defence having the right to the last speech at the trial. Moreover, the defendant cannot himself be questioned unless he consents to be sworn as a witness in his own defence. The right to cross-examine him, even when he is so sworn, is limited by law, with the object of excluding inquiry into his character or into past offences not relevant to the particular charge on which he is being tried. Furthermore, although confessions made in the course of previous judicial proceedings are admissible as evidence if they have been made on oath, no confessions made in any other circumstances are admitted unless it can be proved that they were made voluntarily.

In criminal trials by jury (see below) the judge determines questions of law, sums up the evidence for the benefit of the jury, and acquits the accused or passes sentence according to the verdict of the jury. The jury alone, however, decides the issue of guilt or innocence. Verdicts need not necessarily be unanimous; in certain circumstances the jury may bring in a majority verdict provided that, in the normal jury of 12 people, there are not more than two dissentients.

If the jury returns a verdict of 'not guilty', the prosecution has no right of appeal and the defendant cannot be tried again for the same offence. From a verdict of 'guilty' there is a special right of appeal on the part of the defendant to the appropriate court. The defence or prosecution may suggest that the mental state of the defendant is such that he is unfit to be tried. A jury must decide whether this is so; if they find that it is, the defendant will be admitted to a hospital specified by the Home Secretary.

In Scottish trials on indictment, the first 'pleading' proceedings take place in the sheriff court, when the accused person is called upon to plead guilty or not guilty. If he pleads not guilty, the case is continued to the second 'trial' proceedings in the appropriate court. If he pleads guilty, and it is a case which is to be dealt with in the sheriff court, the sheriff may dispose of it at once. If it is a High Court case it is continued to the second proceedings in the High Court for disposal.

The second proceedings are held at least nine days after the pleading proceedings, either before the sheriff or the High Court, with a jury of 15 members. Evidence is led (without opening speeches), and there are closing speeches for the prosecution and the defence, followed by the judge's charge to the jury. The jury may return a verdict of 'not guilty' or 'not proven', both of which result in acquittal, or they may find the accused 'guilty', in which case the court proceeds to deliver sentence. The verdict may be by a simple majority. Fairness to the accused is ensured by the fact that, with a few minor exceptions, no person may be convicted without the evidence of at least two witnesses, or corroboration of one witness by facts and circumstances which clearly implicate the accused in the crime.

At summary trials in Scotland the accused is asked to plead to the charge at the first calling of the case, and, if he pleads guilty, the court may dispose of the case. Where the plea is 'not guilty', the court may proceed to trial at once or it may appoint a later date.

Juries

In England and Wales a jury summoned to a criminal court consists of 12 people. In Scotland it comprises 15 people; and in Northern Ireland 12 jurors sit in ordinary criminal cases. Jury service in England and Wales is determined by a qualification based on the electoral register: most citizens between the ages of 18 and 65 years are, subject to a five-year residence qualification, eligible for jury service. People following certain occupations are, however, either ineligible or entitled to claim excusal, and certain people with criminal records are disqualified. Jury service in Scotland, for which citizens aged between 21 and 60 years are eligible, is based on a low property qualification. In Northern Ireland service is based on a qualification system similar to that in England and Wales.

A jury is completely independent of both the judiciary and the executive. In criminal cases the accused can have up to seven jurors (five in Scotland) changed without giving reasons, and both defence and prosecution can object for cause shown (for instance, lack of impartiality), but once members of the jury have been sworn they are protected by law from interference of any kind.

Legal Aid and Advice

Legal Advice and Assistance

Before court proceedings are involved, people in England, Wales and Scotland with limited means can obtain help from a solicitor on criminal or civil matters for little or no payment. This includes advice, writing letters, obtaining opinions from a barrister and visiting a police station or prison. Under the scheme a solicitor may act for a client until his costs and expenses reach a total of £25 (authority may be obtained for this limit to be exceeded). A person seeking help has to give the solicitor brief details about his income and savings to show that he comes within the financial limits allowed. People with disposable capital of up to £250 who are also receiving either supplementary benefits or family income supplement are within the financial limits; other people are also eligible provided their disposable capital does not exceed £250 and their weekly disposable income does not exceed £28 (in this case a small contribution may be payable). Similar provisions are proposed for Northern Ireland, where at present representation in criminal trials may be provided free of charge for those with limited means.

Legal Aid

In court proceedings in England and Wales a criminal legal aid order may be made by the court if it appears to be in the interests of justice and that the defendant's means are such that he needs financial help to meet his legal costs. An order must be made when a person is committed for trial on a murder charge or applies for leave to appeal to the House of Lords from the Court of Appeal (Criminal Division). No person can be sentenced for the first time to a custodial sentence unless he is legally represented or, having been informed of his right to apply for legal aid, has been refused or has failed to apply for it.

A criminal legal aid order covers representation of the assisted person by a solicitor and, if necessary, a barrister in all matters relating to the proceedings, including most applications for bail. If the assisted person is unsuccessful in defending the proceedings, his lawyer can advise on the prospects of an appeal against conviction and/or sentence. The applicant may be required by the court to make a financial contribution towards his costs. An order can be granted only to a person charged with a criminal offence, and not to someone seeking to bring a prosecution.

Broadly similar arrangements exist in Scotland, but there is in addition a duty solicitor system which enables people in custody to be represented on first appearing in court without any inquiry into their means.

The Legal Profession

The legal profession in the United Kingdom comprises two distinct branches: solicitors and barristers (advocates in Scotland). Each branch performs its own duties (although certain functions are common to both). Solicitors undertake legal business on behalf of lay clients, while barristers (known collectively as the 'Bar' and collectively and individually as 'counsel') advise on legal problems submitted through solicitors, and present cases in the higher courts. Although the law allows an individual to conduct his own case if he wishes, most people prefer to be legally represented in the more serious court cases. The professional organisations for solicitors and barristers in England and Wales are The Law Society and The Senate of the Inns of Court and the Bar, respectively. The corresponding bodies in Scotland are The Law Society of Scotland and The Faculty of Advocates; in Northern Ireland they are The Incorporated Law Society of Northern Ireland and The Bar Council of Northern Ireland.

TREATMENT OF OFFENDERS

THE CHIEF aims of the penal systems of the United Kingdom are to deter the potential law-breaker and to reform the convicted offender. The element of deterrence is intended to lie in the fear of detection, public trial and possibility of punishment rather than in the severity of the punishment itself.

Penalties

Imprisonment and, for certain categories of young offender, other forms of custodial treatment form an important part of British penal practice, but they are increasingly seen as the last resort in dealing with people who break the law. Wherever possible and appropriate for the safety of the public and the rehabilitation of the individual, the treatment of offenders within the community is regarded as preferable to custodial penalties.

Courts have over the past 20 years made proportionately less and less use of prison as a penalty for adults. Despite this, there has been an increase in the prison population during this period as a result of the underlying rise in crime. Successive governments have encouraged the trend towards less use of imprisonment by introducing legislation to restrict its use for certain groups of offenders, by allowing the conditional suspension of some shorter prison sentences and making available a wider range of alternative non-custodial treatment. In England and Wales the number of men aged 21 and over received into custody for indictable and similar offences per 1,000 men found guilty of indictable offences was 171 in 1972, compared with 357 in 1953.

The trend towards non-custodial treatment has been particularly influenced by three main concerns. The first stems from reservations about the extent to which imprisonment can be said to 'succeed': the efficacy of imprisonment should be reflected in declining reconviction rates among people who have undergone custodial treatment, but research does not in fact indicate this, except for first offenders. The second factor is the high, and increasing, financial cost of keeping a person in prison—an average of over £40 a week in 1974; capital costs probably add at least half as much again, and there are less direct costs such as social security benefits for a prisoner's family. Thirdly, there are the humanitarian aspects and the social cost of imprisonment in terms of the disruption of family life, the dangers of 'institutionalisation' and the severing of such ties with the community as the offender may have.

Traditional non-custodial penalties include fines; probation; absolute or (in England, Wales and Northern Ireland) conditional discharge[1] for up to three years (one year in Northern Ireland); and 'binding over', under which an offender is required to pledge money, with or without sureties, 'to keep the peace and be of good behaviour'.

The suspended sentence in England, Wales and Northern Ireland means that an offender does not actually serve his sentence unless he commits a further offence punishable with imprisonment within a specified period (maximum two years). If a crime is committed within the period of a suspended

---

[1]A discharge is made in circumstances in which there is properly a conviction but the court feels that there is no need to impose punishment.

sentence, the sentence will normally take effect and a further sentence may be imposed for the new offence. An offender who is given a suspended sentence of over six months may, in England and Wales, be made subject to a supervision order for all or part of the period during which the sentence is suspended.

Important advances in the trend towards non-custodial penalties were made in England and Wales by the Criminal Justice Act 1972 (many of the provisions of which have since been consolidated in the Powers of Criminal Courts Act 1973). Offenders who are guilty of imprisonable offences may be ordered to perform a specified number of hours of unpaid service to the community, and there are new provisions for probation hostels and day training centres. An offender may also have his sentence deferred for up to six months with his consent to enable a court to arrive at the most appropriate sentence, taking into account the offender's conduct after, for instance, some expected change in his circumstances. The courts may order an offender to pay compensation for any personal injury, loss or damage resulting from his offence and, in certain circumstances, may order the forfeiture of property used, or intended for use, in the commission of a crime. In the case of major crimes against property a criminal bankruptcy order against the offender can form the basis of bankruptcy proceedings against him. An offender convicted of a serious crime may be disqualified from driving if a motor vehicle was used in its commission. In Scotland a special committee is considering the potential role of the criminal court in achieving reparation by the offender to the victim.

Where an offender needs psychiatric treatment and satisfactory arrangements are available in the community or in hospital, the court may in appropriate cases deal with him by conditional or absolute discharge. Psychiatric treatment in the community or in hospital may also be provided as a condition of a probation order. An offender whom a court considers to be in need of psychiatric treatment may also be compulsorily admitted to hospital (with or without restriction on discharge) or entrusted to the guardianship of a local authority. Psychiatric care is provided by the prison medical service for offenders made subject to the usual custodial sentences, and in appropriate cases transfers are made to National Health Service hospitals.

In 1971 a Government working party recommended that a number of experimental detoxification centres should be established to provide for habitually drunken offenders an alternative to existing ineffective penal measures.[1] A person found drunk and incapable or disorderly in a public place could, instead of being brought before a court, be taken by the police or other agencies to a centre to be 'dried out'. While there, his needs would be assessed by a medical and social work team, and plans would be made for his further treatment, care or support in the community. The Department of Health and Social Security is hoping that two or three experimental centres will be set up in England in due course, and research into the viability of such a centre is taking place in Edinburgh. It is not envisaged that the centres will operate with new compulsory powers, but, if an offender left without receiving treatment, he would remain liable to be charged with an offence.

---

[1] *Habitual Drunken Offenders*, HMSO, 1971, £1·20, ISBN 0 11 340360 7.

The mandatory penalty for murder in the United Kingdom is imprisonment for life.[1] A life sentence is also the maximum penalty which may be imposed for manslaughter and certain other offences, including rape, some robbery and arson.

Except in cases of murder (and of one or two rarely prosecuted offences), for which the penalty is prescribed by law, the judges who preside at the offender's trial have discretion to select the most suitable penalty in the light of the nature and gravity of the offence and the information available about the character and needs of the offender. In certain cases this discretion is modified by statutory provisions designed for the most part to ensure that prison sentences are kept to a minimum. There are special provisions for dealing with children in trouble (see p 46) and with young adult offenders (see p 49).

In England and Wales a person who has not previously served a custodial sentence of a particular kind may not be sentenced to custodial treatment of that kind unless he is legally represented or has chosen not to be, and unless the court is satisfied that no other sentence will suffice. On the other hand, special sentences of somewhat longer duration (extended sentences) may be imposed on persistent offenders.

In Northern Ireland special temporary procedures are provided for dealing with people suspected of terrorism, but there are safeguards for the individual

Table 5

PEOPLE SENTENCED AT MAGISTRATES' COURTS, BY SEX AND SENTENCE OR ORDER: ENGLAND AND WALES 1973

Sentence or order	Males		Females	
	No.	%	No.	%
Absolute discharge	2,516	1·0	612	1·4
Conditional discharge	29,370	11·7	8,497	20·0
Probation	13,271	5·3	5,465	12·9
Supervision order	13,932	5·6	1,987	4·7
Fine	140,976	56·3	22,762	53·7
Detention centre	4,968	2·0	—	—
Care order	5,822	2·3	766	1·8
Suspended sentence	10,730	4·3	1,051	2·5
Imprisonment (immediate)	8,261	3·3	419	1·0
Attendance centre	6,676	2·7	—	—
Committal to Crown Court	10,300	4·1	407	0·9
Otherwise dealt with	3,437	1·0	447	1·1
TOTAL	250,259	100·0	42,413	100·0

Source: *Criminal Statistics 1973.*

[1]The death penalty has not applied for murder in England, Wales and Scotland since 1965 and in Northern Ireland since 1973.

based on referral to independent legal commissioners with a further right of appeal to a tribunal.

Table 5 shows the people found guilty at magistrates' courts of indictable offences in England and Wales in 1973, by sex and court sentence or order. People sentenced at the Crown Court in 1973, including those found guilty at magistrates' courts and committed to the Crown Court for sentence, are shown in Table 6.

Table 6

PEOPLE SENTENCED AT THE CROWN COURT, BY SEX AND SENTENCE OR ORDER: ENGLAND AND WALES 1973

Sentence or order	Males		Females	
	No.	%	No.	%
Conditional discharge	1,749	3·3	333	10·4
Probation	4,180	7·8	913	28·6
Supervision order	270	0·5	35	1·1
Detention centre	2,692	5·1	—	—
Care order	171	0·3	24	0·8
Fine	9,429	17·7	465	14·5
Borstal training	6,578	12·3	212	6·6
Suspended sentence ..	8,493	15·9	562	17·6
Imprisonment (immediate) ..	17,522	32·8	462	14·5
Otherwise dealt with	2,311	4·3	189	5·9
TOTAL	53,395	100·0	3,195	100·0

Source: *Criminal Statistics 1973.*

Administrative Authorities

The Home Secretary and the Secretaries of State for Scotland and Northern Ireland are the Government ministers generally responsible for legislation relating to the treatment of offenders, for collecting statistical and other information about the operation of penal systems, for keeping penal methods under review and for bringing information about these methods to the attention of the courts. In England and Wales the Home Secretary is assisted by an Advisory Council on the Penal System which makes recommendations on matters relating to the prevention of crime and the treatment of offenders. The Scottish Council on Crime keeps under review questions relating to the prevention of crime and the treatment of offenders in Scotland, in consultation with the Secretary of State.

In England and Wales probation, the after-care of prisoners and other related functions are the responsibility of the probation and after-care service. Staff of the service (probation officers) are employed by local probation and after-care committees composed largely of magistrates and representatives of the Crown Court. At a national level the Home Secretary is responsible to Parliament for the efficiency of the service, and has wide regulatory powers.

The Home Office probation and after-care department includes a probation inspectorate which advises and helps local officers and reviews the administration of the service at a local level. Periodic reports are published by the Home Office describing the work of the department (see Reading List, p 56). An independent Advisory Council for Probation and After-Care advises the Home Secretary on the general organisation and development of the service. In Northern Ireland the Secretary of State has responsibility for the probation and after-care service. There is no separate Scottish probation service; local authority social work departments provide the services and officers required by the criminal courts in their areas.

Prison policy and the administration of custodial centres are functions of the Home Office Prison Department, the Scottish Home and Health Department's Prison Service and the Prison Administration of the Northern Ireland Office. Annual reports are published on the work of the Prison Department and the Scottish Prison Service (see Reading List, p 56). A board of visitors composed of men and women representing the local community and including a proportion of magistrates is appointed by the Home Secretary at each prison, remand centre, borstal and detention centre in England and Wales. The boards have a general responsibility to satisfy themselves about the state of the buildings, the administration of the establishment and the treatment of inmates. They report annually to the Home Secretary. They have certain disciplinary powers in relation to serious breaches of discipline, they hear applications or complaints from inmates, and they provide a valuable contact between the local community and the establishment. Similar arrangements exist in Scotland and Northern Ireland. The Home Secretary and the Secretary of State for Scotland are advised by Government-appointed Parole Boards on the release of prisoners on licence (see p 41).

Special provisions within the penal system apply to young offenders. The responsible Government departments are: in England and Wales, the Home Office and the Department of Health and Social Security; in Scotland, the Home and Health and the Education Departments; and, in Northern Ireland, the Northern Ireland Office. Local authority social services departments are responsible for many functions relating to children and young people.

The Probation and After-Care Service

The probation and after-care service and its local authority equivalent in Scotland form a key part of modern penal policy in Britain. The service has a role as a rehabilitative and controlling agency dealing with all kinds of offenders, and provides social work service for the criminal (and civil) courts and penal institutions. It provides a welfare service in prisons and other custodial establishments (see p 44) and of an after-care service for offenders released from penal institutions (see p 45).

The probation officer forms a link through which offenders can be helped to resume their place in society to the benefit of the community as a whole. At the end of 1973 there were 123,000 offenders under the supervision of probation officers in England and Wales—more than three times the total number of offenders in all types of custodial establishments.

Probation Orders

Criminal courts can make a probation order for any offender (in England and Wales, of at least 17 years of age) found guilty of any offence (other than an offence for which there is a fixed penalty). Since co-operation between the offender and the probation officer is a cardinal feature of the system, the offender's consent to an order must be obtained. The court must explain in ordinary language exactly what is involved, and must be sure that the offender understands that if he fails to comply with the terms of the order he may be dealt with for the original offence, or (if the order is allowed to continue) fined up to £50 or ordered to undertake some form of community service. Probation is not, in the legal sense, a sentence in England and Wales, and cannot be made the subject of an appeal against sentence.

An order normally requires the offender to be supervised by a probation officer for a specified period of one year to three years; to be of good behaviour; and to lead an industrious life. It may also require him to submit to treatment for his mental condition, or to live in a specified place such as an approved hostel.

Traditionally a means by which a probation officer can 'advise, assist and befriend' an offender, probation also contains an element of control. It is a form of professional treatment within the community, serving to protect society as well as to aid the offender. Probation supervision is very flexible, and an officer can use it as seems appropriate for each individual case. Whether by regular meetings on an individual basis, by working within the offender's family or by holding discussion groups for several offenders (and sometimes their families), the officer is expected to create the relationship necessary for understanding the offender. If necessary, this also includes careful appraisal of his personality, family, problems and capacities, so as to establish a basis for rehabilitation.

Probation Hostels. To help more immature or inadequate offenders to respond to probation in an initially stable and supportive environment, courts in England and Wales can include in a probation order a requirement for residence in a special 'probation hostel'. The resident is expected to find employment outside the hostel, and from his earnings contributes towards his keep.

Probation hostels have traditionally been provided and managed by voluntary organisations (with Home Office approval), and have catered only for youths and girls.[1] However, a major Home Office programme to develop probation hostels for adult offenders is intended to provide some 1,650 places by 1976–77. So that these hostels should be more closely linked with the probation service, they are being provided by local probation and after-care committees.

Intensive Supervision. Under the code name *Impact*, experiments in various forms of intensive supervision of offenders on probation with particularly difficult problems in their families, work or leisure are being carried out in five areas. Probation officers tend in any case to give more time to their more difficult and demanding clients, but *Impact* is an organised attempt at

---

[1]The results of a Home Office Research Unit study of approved probation hostels for boys were published in 1971 in *Hostels for Probationers*, HMSO, £1·15, ISBN 0 11 340106 X.

intensive treatment in which officers intervene directly in an offender's problems, and make greater use of other resources such as ancillaries, volunteers and other agencies. The results of the experiments will be compared with the results achieved by a 'control group' receiving normal supervision.

Day Training Centres. Under experimental schemes set up to test new provisions introduced in the Criminal Justice Act 1972, courts in four areas of England and Wales have power, with an offender's consent, to attach to his probation order a requirement that he attend, for up to 60 days, a day training centre providing social education linked with intensive probation supervision. The idea is to help the inadequate recidivist whose general social incompetence tends to lead to a succession of short custodial sentences which offer little opportunity for constructive training. It is hoped that day training centres will be particularly appropriate where an offender is unemployed or has difficulty in keeping a steady job.

Offenders attend on a full-time basis five days a week. The centres are staffed by probation officers, and draw upon teachers and others with specialist qualifications to assist. Training programmes include such items as group counselling, remedial education, instruction in home budgeting, and simple work training in woodwork, decorating or car maintenance.

Money Payment Supervision Orders

To help to ensure that a fine or other money owed to a magistrates' court is paid properly, an offender can be placed under the supervision of a probation officer (or other suitable person). No offender under 21 years of age can be sent to prison for the non-payment of a fine unless such an order has been made or the court feels that an order is undesirable or impracticable.

Social Inquiry Reports

To help courts to decide the best possible way of dealing with cases in the interests of both offenders and the community, probation officers at the request of the courts prepare social inquiry reports on the social and domestic background of many accused people, their character, personality, education and employment. This work forms an increasingly important aspect of probation service functions.

An inquiry must be made, in other than trivial cases, if the accused is under the age of 17, and it is normal practice for the court to order one before deciding to commit an offender to a higher court for sentence, before sentencing to imprisonment for a period of up to two years an offender who has not previously been in prison, or before sentencing a young adult offender or a woman to any form of custodial treatment. If an offender is given a custodial sentence, copies of the inquiry report on him are sent to the custodial establishment concerned to indicate any special problems and assist in arrangements for treatment. When a prisoner is eligible for release on parole, a copy of the inquiry report is included in his parole dossier. For a prisoner serving a life sentence, probation officers prepare for the Home Office a special post-sentence social history to supplement any social inquiry report which may have been made.

Means inquiries. If an offender has failed to pay a fine or make some other payment to a court, the court must, before committing him to prison, inquire into his means. It must also make an inquiry into means before making an attachment of earnings order.[1] Probation officers are sometimes asked to help the court by making an investigation into the offender's income and expenditure in these circumstances.

Community Service Orders

The community service order scheme gives the courts a relatively inexpensive alternative to shorter custodial sentences in cases where the need to safeguard the public interest is not an overriding consideration. It provides for offenders aged 17 or over who are convicted of an offence punishable with imprisonment to be ordered, subject to their consent, to carry out in their spare time unpaid work of benefit to the community. The scheme was originally introduced on an experimental basis in six areas, but arrangements are to be made available in other probation and after-care areas in England and Wales. The earliest date for the introduction of the new schemes is 1 April 1975.

The length of an order can vary from 40 to 240 hours, and must be completed within a year. An offender who fails, without reasonable excuse, to comply with the order may be fined up to £50 or dealt with again by the court for his original offence. Run by local probation committees (often with the aid of voluntary agencies and other bodies), the scheme provides offenders with a wide range of tasks, such as helping old and disabled people with painting, decorating and gardening, assisting in youth clubs, building and helping to run adventure playgrounds for children, and providing help in hospitals. Among the offences for which orders were made during the experimental period were theft, burglary, assault, criminal damage, drug offences, handling stolen goods and some traffic offences. Most offenders given community order sentences had had one or more previous convictions; over half were in the 17–20 age group.

Scotland

In Scotland, where there is no separate probation service, local authority social work departments provide the services required by the criminal courts in their areas. Offenders subject to probation orders or to after-care supervision following release from a penal institution are supervised by social workers from these departments.

Prisons

The aims of the prison service are briefly to provide for the detention of those committed to custody under the law in conditions generally acceptable to society, and to develop constructive methods of treatment and training designed to lead to the prisoner's rehabilitation and reform. To this end prisoners are classified into groups, taking into account their escape potential, the degree to which their escape would offer a threat to the public or the State, and the justification of high expenditure on providing secure conditions.

---

[1] A court order which, to enforce, for example, a fine or a legal aid contribution, instructs an employer to make deductions from the earnings of an employee who has defaulted on payment.

Unconvicted prisoners are entitled to privileges not granted to convicted prisoners. As far as practicable, unconvicted prisoners are separated from convicted prisoners, and prisoners under 21 are separated from those over that age (see p 51).

Prisons to which offenders may be committed directly by a court are known as 'local prisons'; all are closed establishments. Other prisons, which may be 'open'[1] or closed, receive prisoners on transfer from local prisons. Or 114 custodial establishments for men and women in England and Wales, 21 are open. Since 1971 there has been a downward trend in the number of people serving sentences in prison. The number of prisoners in custody in prison service establishments[2] in England and Wales in mid-1974 was about 37,000.[2] Separate prisons cater for female prisoners of whom there are about 1,000 at any one time. Many British prisons were built during the nineteenth century when imprisonment became a penalty in itself, and are unsatisfactory by modern standards. Overcrowding is also a problem, with some 3,000 inmates living three to a cell (although the number has dropped from 8,000 in 1971). To improve conditions generally and to relieve overcrowding, new prisons are being built and existing establishments redeveloped and modernised.

Remission of Sentence and Parole

All prisoners serving a sentence of imprisonment for an actual term of more than one month are allowed remission of one-third of their sentence provided that this does not reduce their sentence to below 31 days (30 days in Scotland). Remission may be forfeited for serious misconduct in prison.

In addition, all prisoners in England, Wales and Scotland serving fixed sentences totalling more than 18 months become eligible for consideration for early release on 'parole' after serving one-third of their sentence or 12 months, whichever expires later. Under this scheme a prisoner continues his sentence in the community outside prison, subject to the supervision of a probation officer, and must comply with conditions laid down in the licence for his release (relating, for instance, to place of residence). Failure to comply with any condition in the licence, or any other unsatisfactory behaviour, may result in recall to prison. The licence remains in force until the date on which the prisoner would have been released (with remission) if he had not been granted parole or, for prisoners serving extended sentences and young prisoners, until the end of the sentence. Of those eligible for consideration, the ratio of offenders granted parole to those who complete the balance of their sentence (less remission) in prison is roughly 2 : 3. The average period on parole is about eight months. There is a local review committee at each prison.

Every eligible prisoner is first considered for release on parole by the committee which comprises the governor or deputy governor of the prison, members of the board of visitors, probation and after-care officers and independent people. The committees report to the Home Secretary or the

---

[1]'Open prisons' do not have traditional precautions such as outer walls, locks, bars and special guards, and are designed to encourage a sense of responsibility among inmates.
[2]This figure roughly comprises 24,000 people serving prison sentences, 5,700 unsentenced and non-criminal prisoners, 5,600 borstal inmates and 1,800 inmates of detention centres.

Secretary of State for Scotland. In some cases the minister concerned has power to grant parole solely on the committee's recommendation; others he refers to the appropriate Parole Board. There is a Parole Board for England and Wales and another for Scotland. Their members include judges, psychiatrists, senior probation officers, criminologists and laymen. Where the Parole Board recommends favourably, the decision whether or not to release depends finally on the minister, but, where the board does not recommend release, the minister has no power to grant parole.

A system of parole is being considered for Northern Ireland.

Prisoners serving life sentences are also eligible for release on licence. In England, Wales and Scotland the usual practice is to seek the views of the local review committee after the offender has served seven years. Each case is considered by the Home Secretary or the Secretary of State for Scotland and forwarded to the appropriate Parole Board. The Lord Chief Justice (in England and Wales) or the Lord Justice General (in Scotland) and (if he is available) the judge who presided at the offender's trial must be consulted before any life sentence prisoner is released. In Northern Ireland the judiciary is similarly consulted before any such release takes place. Prisoners released in this way remain on licence for the whole of their lives, and are therefore subject to recall at any time should the circumstances warrant it.

Employment

The main aim of prison industries is to give an offender in custody a training and experience that will fit him to get and retain a job on discharge. The primary source of work lies in the domestic requirements of the prison service in clothing and equipping prisoners and providing furniture and soft furnishings for the establishments. Goods and services are also supplied to other Government departments and public bodies, and there is a steady growth of sales of a wide range of products in the open market—for example, textiles, woodwork and engineering products.

The profitable farming and horticultural industries also provide a useful source of work for inmates, and, apart from normal commercial industries, play an increasing part in contributing to the prison food provision. A small number of prisoners are employed outside prison in agriculture and on work such as archaeological excavation and land reclamation.

In England, Wales and Scotland small payments are made to inmates for the work they do; in some prisons special incentive schemes provide an opportunity for higher earnings on the basis of output and skill. In Northern Ireland there is a progressive system of earnings, related to work done.

Any prisoner serving a sentence of four years or more may be considered for employment in an ordinary civilian job outside prison for about six months before his discharge. Prisoners selected for the scheme live either in a separate part of the prison or in a prison hostel; they are paid normal wages, from which they support their families and meet their own expenses.

Education

Education for those in custody is provided by local education authorities in close liaison with central education departments. Each prison in England and Wales has an education officer, a number of part-time teachers and, increasingly nowadays, one or more full-time teachers. Prisoners may attend evening classes and take correspondence courses when these are available. Other educational facilities—such as physical training, concerts, plays, films, lectures and group discussions—are arranged where facilities allow; prisoners may also use the prison libraries, which depend largely upon the local public libraries for their stocks. Selected prisoners undertake vocational training courses, leading to an acknowledged qualification. Training in construction industry crafts is also given to certain prisoners. On completion of training their newly acquired skills are put to use in building new, and in maintaining and improving existing, establishments. Experiments with Open University studies,[1] full-time education and day-release from prison work for study are being carried out. Prisons in Scotland and Northern Ireland provide educational facilities similar to those in England and Wales.

Physical Education

The purpose of physical education in prison establishments is to maintain and improve general physical fitness. Instructors are recruited and trained from among interested prison officers. Physical education has long traditions in borstals, and plays a vital part in the more recently created detention centres. All offenders under 21 years have to attend a certain number of day-time physical education classes a week, but adults are free to choose whether to take part or not.

Medical Services

The statutory duty of the prison medical officer is the care, physical and mental, of prison inmates. Large establishments have medical teams, while small ones may only need the services of a medical officer on a part-time basis. All have appropriate hospital and out-patient treatment facilities and the necessary support staff.

In selected prisons major surgery with National Health Service consultants and specialist services is available for patients, including those from other establishments who for several reasons cannot be transferred to National Health Service surgical units. There is one psychiatric prison in England and Wales with accommodation for some 325 people. Several establishments provide psychiatric services, and prisoners are transferred from other establishments to benefit from them. Full use is made wherever possible of hospital and out-patient facilities of the National Health Service, and, if necessary, arrangements are made for treatment to continue after release from custody.

Psychological Services

The psychologist's role in the penal system is one of applying psychological techniques so as to help in the task of making the system more effective. Psychologists are engaged in a variety of activities determined to some extent by the institution concerned. Generally they are used by the prison service as specialist resource staff. Many engage in organisational aspects of the

---

[1]The Open University provides degree courses by using a combination of radio, television and correspondence courses together with a network of viewing and listening centres: see COI short note, *Britain's Open University*, SN5923.

service such as advising on management processes within an institution. Some, especially those in remand centres, allocation centres and training prisons, are involved in making clinical assessments of inmates. Advising on, and participating in, treatment programmes for inmates is another area of work, so that some psychologists find their main task concerned both with helping management to design and apply such programmes and with staff training directed towards a greater understanding of the individual or group behaviour of inmates.

Privileges and Discipline

All prisoners, from the beginning of their sentence, have a legal right to write and receive letters and to be visited by their relations at regular intervals. They also have such privileges as additional letters and visits, the use of books, periodicals and newspapers, and the right to make purchases from the canteen with money they have earned in prison. Depending on the facilities available at individual establishments, they may be granted the further privileges of dining and recreation in association and watching television in the evening.

Breaches of discipline are dealt with by the prison governor, or board of visitors, who have power to order, among other penalties, forfeiture of remission and forfeiture of privileges.

Welfare

Welfare in prisons is the general concern of the prison staff as a whole, and in particular of the chaplains and assistant governors, but special responsibilities attach to prison welfare officers, who, in England, Wales and Northern Ireland, are probation officers seconded by the probation and after-care service (in Scotland social workers from local authority social work departments).

The functions of these officers include helping the prisoner in his relationships with individuals and organisations outside the prison, and making plans for the prisoner's after-care, working closely in this connection with colleagues in the probation and after-care service and with other agencies in the community whose help the prisoner or his family may need either during sentence or after release.

Prisoners may also receive visits from specially appointed prison visitors, whose work is voluntary and in England and Wales is co-ordinated and guided by the National Association of Prison Visitors.

Religion

In the belief that every inmate is entitled to receive spiritual help from a minister of his own religion, every prison establishment in England and Wales has a Church of England chaplain, a Roman Catholic priest and a Methodist minister appointed to it. Representatives of other denominations are called on as required. Church of England chaplains and Roman Catholic priests work full-time in the prison department in England and Wales and, with the ministers of other churches giving full- and part-time service, come under the general oversight of the Chaplain General of Prisons. Church ministers provide a programme of religious education and hold services of worship as their special responsibility, but are increasingly becoming involved in the treatment of offenders generally.

Discharge and After-Care

After-care in fact begins at the commencement of a prisoner's sentence, and probation officers arrange interviews for offenders in the cells at court immediately after sentence. Officers often visit prisoners' families to discuss problems so that, when the time for discharge arrives, difficulties are understood, plans have been made, and the vital relationship between officer, offender and family has already been forged. In some areas the probation service has set up prisoners' wives' groups which meet informally and provide a source of mutual companionship and support.

All prisons in England and Wales arrange for pre-release preparations for prisoners in their care. These vary according to the needs of the prisoners concerned, and at many prisons are in the form of a series of open discussions taken by experts, on domestic, social and employment problems. Home leave, allowing five clear days at home, is extensively granted to prisoners with sentences of two years or over towards the end of their sentences to enable them to make family adjustments and contacts with potential employers.

Further assistance in the task of bridging the gap between prison life and the outside world is provided for selected male prisoners serving four years or more (in Scotland, three years or more) and for women prisoners serving 18 months or more. There are special provisions for some prisoners to work outside the prison prior to their release (see p 42).

There are two systems of after-care for those discharged from custodial treatment in England and Wales. A compulsory system applies to prisoners released from life imprisonment or extended sentences, young prisoners and young people discharged from borstals and detention centres; and a voluntary system is offered to the remainder. Both systems are in the hands of the probation and after-care service which, in the case of the compulsory system, is responsible for seeing that discharged offenders observe the conditions laid down—for instance, that they report to the probation officer during the period of statutory supervision, and that they inform him of any change of address or of place of work.

On discharge a prisoner is provided with necessary clothing and, if he has served a sentence of over 14 days' duration, he may receive a small discharge grant. Every discharged offender also has his fare paid to his destination, and receives subsistence for his journey if he is not given a discharge grant. General responsibility for subsequent financial help to discharged prisoners and their dependants who are without normal means of support rests with the Department of Health and Social Security, which also has power to meet other special needs—for instance, for tools and working clothes. When the department is unable to help, the probation and after-care service may offer financial aid from befriending funds, financed equally by the Home Office and local authorities.

After-care is also provided by a number of voluntary societies, most of which are members of the National Association for the Care and Resettlement of Offenders. This may take the form of providing associates to probation officers in their work of befriending ex-prisoners; befriending prisoners' families; providing club rooms; or helping discharged offenders to find work and lodgings. Voluntary organisations, with some financial assistance from the Home Office, are providing some 1,700 places in some 170 hostels specifically for ex-offenders. Not all men in need of accommodation, however, are willing to live in a hostel, and voluntary bodies also provide self-contained flatlets and bed-sitting rooms with some social work support. Experiments have also been undertaken with the provision of social support work for landladies willing to accommodate offenders.

In Northern Ireland after-care duties are likewise carried out by probation and after-care officers. In Scotland responsibility for statutory and voluntary after-care is vested in social workers from local authority social work departments.

Children in Trouble

No child under 10 years of age can be held criminally responsible in England and Wales. A child aged 10 and under 17 years who is alleged to have committed an offence may be the subject of criminal proceedings or of 'care proceedings' under the provision of the Children and Young Persons Act 1969. The Act contains power to raise the minimum age for criminal proceedings to 14 years (in which case only care proceedings would be available for children aged 10–13).

For many years the philosophy underlying the treatment of children in trouble has increasingly been to blur the distinction between those who have committed an offence and those who are in trouble for some other reason, and this approach is inherent in the 1969 Act. The aims of protecting society from the consequences of juvenile deliquency and of protecting the young and helping them to grow into mature and law-abiding people are seen as complementary rather than as distinct and contradictory. Criminal behaviour in children and young people is regarded less as a problem in itself, to be treated in isolation, than as one of several factors in a child's personality, history and background, the existence of any of which might point to a lack of care or control requiring social intervention.

Juvenile Courts

In England, Wales and Northern Ireland care or criminal proceedings involving children and young people under 17 years of age are held before special types of magistrates' courts known as 'juvenile courts'. The case of a young person charged jointly with someone over 17 is heard in a normal magistrates' court or higher court; if the young person is found guilty and not discharged or fined, the court remits the case to a juvenile court. If a child or young person is charged with an offence which, in the case of an adult, is punishable on indictment with 14 years' imprisonment or more, a juvenile court may commit him for trial in the Crown Court. In the very rare event of a child being charged with homicide, the case is only triable on indictment at the Crown Court, but committal takes place in a juvenile court unless there is a joint charge against a person over 17 years of age.

Juvenile courts exercise their powers subject to the overriding principle of the welfare of the child. They comprise not more than three magistrates—

nearly always including at least one man and one woman drawn from a panel of those most suited to dealing with children—and must sit in a different place from other courts or at a different time. Proceedings are less formal than in an adult court, and the public is excluded. Accredited press representatives may be present, but they are not allowed to publish any details that might lead to the identification of the child unless the court or the Home Secretary expressly dispenses with this requirement in the interests of justice. The courts must explain the substance of the charge or application in language which the child can understand, and parents or guardians may be required to attend during all stages of the proceedings. Having determined the guilt of a young offender on the evidence, the court must, before deciding on a method of treatment, consider any information concerning school record, health, character and home conditions that may be provided by a probation officer or the local authority.

Care Proceedings

To make an order in care proceedings the juvenile court must be satisfied that any one of a number of conditions is met, one of which, in the case of a child or young person over the age of 10 years, is that an offence has been committed. The court must also be of the opinion that the child or young person is in need of care or control which he is unlikely to receive unless an order is made. This means that the commission of an offence is not in itself a ground for a court order. Care proceedings, where an offence is alleged, may be initiated by a local authority or the police if they reasonably believe that there are grounds for making an order.

The following orders are available to the court in both care and criminal proceedings:

(a) A care order committing the child to the care of a local authority. The effect of this type of order is that the local authority has legal custody of the child, and has power to restrict his liberty where necessary. The authority is responsible for deciding where the child should be accommodated—for example, with foster parents or in one of the 'community homes' being provided for all children in care on a regional basis throughout the country.

For children who are too severely disturbed and disruptive to be treated successfully in other child care homes but who do not need treatment in hospital, three new establishments—known as 'youth treatment centres'—are being provided.[1]

(b) A supervision order for a specified period of up to three years. Supervision of a child under 13 years is carried out by a local authority social worker (a probation officer may be appointed if he or she is already working with the child's family). For children aged 13–16 supervision is (at the discretion of the court) by either a social worker or a probation officer. Any one of the following conditions may be attached to a supervision order: (i) a requirement to submit to treat-

---

[1] A guide to this form of treatment for severely disturbed children has been published by the Department of Health and Social Security: *Youth Treatment Centres*, HMSO, 1971, 27½p, ISBN 0 11 320423 X.

ment for a mental condition; (ii) a requirement to reside with a named individual—for example, a relative; or (iii) an 'intermediate treatment' requirement. Intermediate treatment—which is in between those measures which involve complete removal from home and those which do not—consists of participation, under a supervisor, in a variety of constructive and remedial activities either through a short residential course or through attendance at a day or evening centre.[1] The object is to bring the child into contact with a new environment giving an opportunity to develop new interests. Often treatment involves the child with other children who have not been before the courts.

(c) An order requiring the child's parents or guardian to take proper care of him and to exercise proper control over him.

(d) A hospital or guardianship order in accordance with the mental health legislation.

(e) Payment of compensation (an offence must be proved and the maximum amount which can be ordered is £400).

Criminal Proceedings

The following additional orders are available to the courts in criminal proceedings (powers (f) and (g) can be exercised only by the Crown Court)[2]:

(a) Binding over.

(b) Absolute or conditional discharge.

(c) Fines.

(d) Attendance centre order, if the offender is a boy and a centre is available to the court. There are 60 centres in England and Wales for boys between the ages of 10 and 17 found guilty of offences for which older people could be sentenced to imprisonment. Boys ordered to attend must do so during their spare time on Saturdays; they may be required to attend for up to three hours on any one occasion and for a total of not less than 12 hours (with certain exceptions) and not more than 24. The activities include physical training and instruction in handicrafts or some other practical subject. Efforts are made at the centres to induce the boys to join a youth club or other suitable organisation. There are two attendance centres for young men aged 17 and under 21 (see p 51). The one attendance centre in Northern Ireland operates on similar lines, but caters for boys between the ages of 12 and 17.

(e) Detention centre order for boys aged 14 or over (see p 50).

(f) Borstal training if the offender is aged 15 or over (see p 50).

(g) Detention in a place approved by the Home Secretary—this power is only used in the case of very serious crimes.

---

[1] See *Intermediate Treatment Project*, HMSO, 1973, 20p, ISBN 0 11 320305 5.

[2] The Children and Young Persons Act 1969 provides for the eventual withdrawal of the power to send offenders to attendance centres and detention centres (the centres being brought within the system of local authority community homes), and for the raising of the minimum age for borstal training first to 16 and then to 17 years.

Children aged 14 to 16 remanded or committed for trial or sentence are entrusted to the care of a local authority. Those certified by a court to be too unruly for such care are committed to a remand centre (or sometimes a prison). Children aged 15 or 16 who have been convicted and for whom the juvenile court thinks borstal training may be appropriate are (unless released on bail) committed to a remand centre or prison to await sentence by the Crown Court.

Scotland

In Scotland the age of criminal responsibility is eight years, but prosecution is the exception, and no child can be prosecuted for an offence other than at the instance of the Lord Advocate. Children who have committed an offence or need care and protection are generally brought before an informal children's hearing which aims to discuss informally their difficulties, and to provide the most appropriate measures of care and treatment.

Social workers, doctors, friends or neighbours, the child's parents, the police or the local authority may all refer a case to a local authority employee known as the 'reporter', who administers hearings and decides whether cases should be brought before a hearing or not. Investigations can be helped by the police or the local authority social work department.

Each hearing comprises three members of the local community (one of whom must be a woman) from a local panel. The child, his (or her) parent and a representative from the local social work department normally attend, and proceedings are kept as informal as possible.

The hearing may decide that the child needs compulsory measures of care, and commit him to supervision by the local authority, a voluntary organisation or an individual. All aspects of the supervision requirement are discussed with the parents and the child. Conditions appropriate to the child's needs may be attached to the requirement—these may include, for example, residence away from home, participation in recreational activities or evening classes, or help for the aged or handicapped.

Other powers of children's hearings include reporting to the local education authority that a child may have special educational needs, and reporting to the local mental health officer that a child may need hospital treatment.

Young Adult Offenders

This section describes the existing powers of the courts to deal with offenders aged 17 and under 21, and the treatment facilities available. The recognition of young adult offenders as a category distinct from child and adult offenders has existed in the United Kingdom since the beginning of the century.

About a quarter of all offenders found guilty of indictable offences in England and Wales come from within this category, and they comprise about the same proportion of the average sentenced population of custodial penal establishments. Seventeen is the age at which the proportion of the population found guilty of indictable offences reaches its peak: in 1972 it was over 6 per cent of young men of that age.

A major report on the treatment of young adult offenders, published in May 1974 by the Home Secretary's Advisory Council on the Penal System, recommended new initiatives to enable more young adult offenders to be dealt with in the community rather than in custody (see p 52).

Custodial Sentences

The custodial sentences available to the courts are: detention in a detention centre, 'borstal' training[1] and imprisonment. Detention centre and borstal training are also used for offenders under 17 years.

For detention centres there are separate committal arrangements and separate centres for offenders aged 17 and over and for those aged under 17; there is no such distinction in the borstal system.

Detention Centres. Detention centres provide a means of treating young male offenders for whom a long period of residential training away from home does not seem necessary or justified by the offence, but who cannot be taught respect for the law by such non-custodial measures as fines or probation. In England and Wales there are 12 senior detention centres providing accommodation for up to 1,400 trainees (as well as six junior centres for boys aged 14–16 years). Detention may be for a period of three months (minimum) to six months; if consecutive sentences are passed, the total term must not exceed six months, or nine months in certain exceptional cases. A trainee is allowed remission of one-third of his sentence which may be forfeited for misbehaviour. In Scotland, where there is only one senior centre, the fixed period for all detention centre sentences is three months and the age range is from 16 to 20 years. There are no detention centres in Northern Ireland.

The regime in a detention centre is brisk and formal, demanding the highest possible standard of discipline and achievement. An offender must be medically examined and found fit for the life in a centre. The keynote is positive treatment in a routine which, in the senior centre, provides a normal working week of 40 hours, including one hour each day devoted to physical education, with increasing attention paid to education provided mainly by evening classes. Boys of compulsory school age in the junior centres receive full-time education. All young offenders discharged from a detention centre are subject to statutory supervision for a year.

Borstal Training. The borstal training system is available for offenders aged 15–20 years (16–20 years in Scotland and 16–21 years in Northern Ireland). Allocation to particular borstals used to be based on such criteria as age, intelligence and criminal sophistication, but the emphasis has moved towards keeping the offender as near his home area as possible so as to maintain and foster his ties with the local community. Courts rarely order borstal training unless they have tried fines, probation or detention centre training, perhaps all three, and it is primarily intended for offenders of at least 17 years of age. In England, Wales and Northern Ireland the period of training ranges from six months to two years, and is followed by supervision for two years (one year in Northern Ireland). The actual term of a boy's custodial care depends on his response to training. On average it is less than a year. In Scotland, where there is no minimum period of training, the maximum is two years, and the supervision period lasts for one year.

Borstal training aims at bringing about a development in the trainee's

---

[1] The name derives from the place in Kent where the first institution of this kind was established.

character and capacities, progressively providing increasing scope for personal decision, responsibility and self-control, and enabling the trainee to develop as an individual. The daily routine generally includes a 40-hour working week with opportunities for suitable trainees to undertake vocational training or construction industry training courses, physical education, general education at evening classes, and recreation. Outside activities are encouraged and services provided to the community are increasing. There is considerable freedom of movement, and many borstals are open establishments.

Imprisonment. A person aged under 17 years cannot be sentenced to imprisonment, and no court may pass a sentence of imprisonment on an offender aged 17–20 years unless satisfied that no other method of dealing with him is appropriate. If imprisonment is imposed, the term must normally be of not more than six months or less than three years (or 18 months if the person has served a previous sentence of not less than six months' imprisonment or a sentence of borstal training). Sentences of up to two years may be ordered by a court, as in the case of adult offenders, to be suspended.

Prisoners under the age of 21 at the time of their sentence are classified as young prisoners and serve their sentence separately from older prisoners unless they are reclassified as adults and treated as such in an adult prison. Reclassification, which depends on their degree of maturity or criminal sophistication, may be effected when they reach the age of 18, but for many does not take place until they reach the age of 21. Most young prisoners serving medium- and long-term sentences go to one of six young prisoners' centres—allocation is as far as possible on the basis of proximity to home— while those with short sentences mostly remain at their local prison in accommodation separate from older prisoners. A few go to remand centres as members of working parties providing domestic and maintenance services. Remission is granted at the normal prison rate of one-third.

All young offenders, whether or not reclassified as adults, are subject to statutory supervision and after-care on release. Those sentenced to less than 18 months are under supervision for 12 months, while those sentenced to 18 months or more, if not released on parole as in the case of adults (see p 41), are under supervision until the end of the sentence.

A person found guilty of murder who was under the age of 18 when the crime was committed must be sentenced to detention 'during Her Majesty's pleasure'. Offenders subject to this sentence, or to life imprisonment, may be released on licence (see p 42).

In Scotland no offender under 21 years may be sent to prison. Where neither borstal nor detention centre training is suitable for an offender aged 16–20, detention in a special 'young offenders institution' may be ordered.

Non-custodial Sentences

The main non-custodial measures used in dealing with young adults are generally the same as those used in dealing with adults—that is to say, absolute and conditional discharge, binding over, fines, probation and, in some areas, community service. An additional measure, available only to courts in the Greater London and Manchester areas, is the attendance centre order, which is more commonly used for younger boys (see p 48).

Advisory Council's Proposals

In a 1974 report, *Young Adult Offenders* (see Reading List, p 56), the Home Secretary's Advisory Council on the Penal System set out its findings following a thorough review of the methods of treatment of offenders in this age group in England and Wales. The council's terms of reference asked for particular attention to be paid to treatment in custody, and many of its main recommendations relate to the extent of reliance on custodial methods in dealing with young offenders and on a new sentencing framework.

The basic theme of the report is that there should be a shift in emphasis away from treatment in custody and towards treatment in the community. This change would involve both dealing with a higher proportion of young offenders wholly within the community, and, when committal to custody is necessary, retaining offenders' links with the community and returning them to it as soon as practicable. To achieve this aim the council proposes two new forms of sentence: one with a partially custodial element—the 'custody and control order' which would replace existing custodial sentences for young adults—and the other essentially non-custodial—the 'supervision and control order'.

Dealing with the custody and control order, the council emphasises flexible release procedures, followed by supervision and control in the community for all offenders in this age group on whom custodial sentences have been imposed. New machinery would be required to review individual cases with a view to their early release under supervision, and there would also be a need for added resources for supervision in the community.

The proposed supervision and control order would be operated by the probation service, and would exist alongside the normal probation order, which with other existing non-custodial measures would still be available to the courts. The council's intention in recommending the new order is to enable the courts to retain a wider range of young adult offenders under supervision in the community, on the bases that there would be closer supervision than is commonly provided under a probation order, and that the order gives the supervising officer a wide range of requirements, the activation of which would be at his discretion (these might include requirements of employment, residence and education or work training).

The Home Secratary has welcomed the broad approach of the report, and is considering its detailed proposals in consultation with the probation and after-care and prison services and other organisations involved with young adult offenders.

APPENDIX 1

CONTROL OF FIREARMS

In England, Wales and Scotland the Firearms Act 1968 sets out a series of graded controls over the acquisition and possession of firearms.[1] Weapons fall into four main categories:

(a) Prohibited weapons such as machine guns, sub-machine guns and weapons designed for the discharge of noxious gases or liquids—for the possession, manufacture, sale or acquisition of which the authority of the Home Secretary or the Secretary of State for Scotland is required.

(b) Rifles, pistols, most of their ammunition, short-barrelled shot guns (those with a barrel less than 24 inches (60·96 cm) in length) and specially dangerous air weapons. A firearm certificate issued by the local chief officer of police is required for the acquisition or possession of individual weapons of this sort. The officer must be satisfied that an applicant for a certificate has good reason for having the firearm and is fit to be entrusted with it, and that the public safety or peace will not be endangered. Conditions may be attached to the certificate—a standard one on all certificates requires weapons and ammunition to be kept in a secure place except when in use. There is a right of appeal to a court against the refusal of a certificate.

(c) Shot guns. A certificate from the local chief officer of police is required for the acquisition or possession of long-barrelled shot guns. Other than in the case of people prohibited from possessing firearms of any kind, the grant of a certificate can be refused only if public safety or the peace would be endangered by granting it. There is a right of appeal to a court against a refusal. One certificate authorises the possession of an unlimited number of shot guns; there is no condition requiring safe keeping, and ammunition is not controlled.

(d) Air weapons, except those classified as specially dangerous, are not subject to certificate control, although there are some general restrictions on their possession and use by young people under 17 years of age.

The 1968 Act specifically prohibits the possession of firearms by a person who has served a lengthy prison sentence—for life if the sentence was for three years or more, for five years if it was for between three months and three years. (An application can be made to a court to have this prohibition set aside). The Act also provides for a number of special exemptions from the certificate requirement. The more important are that a member of a rifle club or cadet corps approved by the Home Secretary or the Secretary of State for Scotland may possess a firearm, without a certificate, when engaged in target practice or drill as a member; and a person manning a miniature rifle range or gallery with ·22 rifles may acquire and possess such rifles, without a certificate, and anyone may use such a gun at the range or gallery.

Firearms or ammunition dealers must be registered with the police, and must keep detailed records of their business. In general, registration can be refused (an appeal can be made to a court against a refusal) only if the business proposed would present a danger to public safety or the peace.

---

[1]This summary is extracted from a consultative document, *The Control of Firearms in Great Britain*, published by the then Government in May 1973: Cmnd 5297, HMSO, 52½p, ISBN 0 10 152970 8.

The Act also lays down heavy maximum penalties for certain criminal uses of firearms, and these penalties have been increased by the Criminal Justice Act 1972.

Offences of possessing a firearm with intent to endanger life, or of using a firearm to resist arrest, carry a maximum penalty of life imprisonment. Offences of carrying a firearm to commit an indictable offence, or while committing certain specified offences, carry a maximum penalty of 14 years' imprisonment.

The holder of a firearm or shot gun may import his weapon into England, Wales and Scotland on production of his certificate. If he has no certificate, an import licence obtainable from the Import Licensing Board of the Department of Trade (Sanctuary Buildings, 16–20 Great Smith Street, London SW1P 3DB) is required, but he cannot take possession of the weapon until he has obtained the necessary certificate from the police. A visitor who does not intend to stay for more than 30 days in any 12 months does not need a certificate or import licence for a shot gun in his possession.

Northern Ireland

Controls in Northern Ireland are set out in the Firearms Act (Northern Ireland) 1968.

For 'prohibited weapons' such as machine guns, certain self-loading rifles and weapons designed to discharge noxious gases or liquids, the Home Secretary's authority is required for possession, manufacture, sale or acquisition.

The acquisition or possession of all other weapons and their ammunition (including rifles, pistols, revolvers, shot guns and air weapons) is subject to the issue of a firearms certificate by the Chief Constable of the Royal Ulster Constabulary.

Visitors from outside the United Kingdom who wish to bring firearms into Northern Ireland should first contact the Chief Constable of the Royal Ulster Constabulary, Headquarters, Brooklyn, Knock Road, Belfast BT5 6LE.

APPENDIX 2

LIST OF ORGANISATIONS

GOVERNMENT DEPARTMENTS

Home Office, Whitehall, London SW1A 2AP.

Lord Chancellor's Office, House of Lords, London SW1A 0PW.

Law Officers' Department, Attorney General's Chambers, Royal Courts of Justice, Strand, London WC2A 2LL.

Department of Health and Social Security, Alexander Fleming House, London SE1 6BY.

Scottish Home and Health Department, St Andrew's House, Edinburgh EH1 3DE.

Lord Advocate's Department, Fielden House, 10 Great College Street, London SW1P 3SL.

Crown Office, 9 Parliament Square, Edinburgh EH1 1RH.

Northern Ireland Office, Stormont Castle, Belfast BT4 3ST.

OTHER ORGANISATIONS

The Bar Council of Northern Ireland, Royal Courts of Justice, Belfast.

Criminal Injuries Compensation Board, 10–12 Russell Square, London WC1B 5EN.

Criminal Law Revision Committee, c/o Home Office, Whitehall, London SW1A 2AP.

The Faculty of Advocates, Parliament House, Parliament Square, Edinburgh EH1 1RF.

Howard League for Penal Reform, 125 Kennington Park Road, London SE11 4JP.

Incorporated Law Society of Northern Ireland, Royal Courts of Justice, Belfast.

Justice (the British Section of the International Commission of Jurists), 12 Crane Court, Fleet Street, London EC4A 2JJ.

Law Commission, Conquest House, 37–38 John Street, Theobalds Road, London WC1N 2BQ.

The Law Society, 113 Chancery Lane, London WC2A 1PL.

The Law Society of Scotland, 26 Drumsheugh Gardens, Edinburgh EH3 7YR.

Metropolitan Police, New Scotland Yard, Broadway, London SW1H 0BG.

National Association for the Care and Resettlement of Offenders, 125 Kennington Park Road, London SE11 4JP.

National Association of Prison Visitors, 47 Hartington Street, Bedford.

National Council for Civil Liberties, 152 Camden High Street, London NW1 0NE.

Scottish Association for the Care and Rehabilitation of Offenders, 1 Strathmore House, East Kilbride.

Scottish Law Commission, Old College, South Bridge, Edinburgh EH8 9BD.

The Senate of the Inns of Court and the Bar, Fountain Court, Temple, London EC4Y 9DQ.

READING LIST

OFFICIAL PUBLICATIONS
(*published by Her Majesty's Stationery Office*)

Annual Reports:
  Commissioner of Police of the Metropolis.
  Criminal Injuries Compensation Board.
  Criminal Statistics (England and Wales).
  Criminal Statistics (Scotland).
  Her Majesty's Chief Inspector of Constabulary.
  Her Majesty's Chief Inspector of Constabulary for Scotland.
  Home Office Prison Department.
  Home Office Prison Department—Statistical Tables.
  Home Office Probation and After-Care Department (reports from time to time).
  Parole Board (England and Wales).
  Parole Board for Scotland.

		£
Prisons in Scotland.		
Intermediate Treatment Project. *ISBN 0 11 320305 5.*	1973	0·20
Prison Service Journal (published quarterly).		0·05
The Probation and After-Care Service in England and Wales. *ISBN 0 11 340376 3.*	1973	0·29
Young Adult Offenders. (A report by the Advisory Council on the Penal System.) *ISBN 0 11 340559 6.*	1974	1·65

OTHER PUBLICATIONS

HALL WILLIAMS, J. E. The English Penal System in Transition. *ISBN 0 406 59311 6* (paperback).	*Butterworths*	1970	3·00
JACKSON, R. M. Enforcing the Law. *ISBN 0 14 021146 2* (paperback).	*Penguin*	1972	0·60
——The Machinery of Justice in England. *ISBN 0 521 08644 2.*	*Cambridge*	1972	5·90
LEIGH, L. H. Police Powers in England and Wales. *ISBN 0 406 84540 9.*	*Butterworths*	1975	5·60
McCLEAN, J. D. *and* WOOD, J. C. Criminal Justice and the Treatment of Offenders. *ISBN 0 421 10170 9.*	*Sweet and Maxwell*	1969	3·50
SMITH, J. C. *and* HOGAN, BRIAN. The Criminal Law. *ISBN 0 406 65805 6* (paperback).	*Butterworths*	1973	4·60
WALKER, NIGEL. Crime and Punishment in Britain. *ISBN 0 85224 038 4.*	*Edinburgh University Press*	1968	2·00
WALKER, PETER N. The Courts of Law: A Guide to their History and Working. *ISBN 0 7153 4977 7.*	*David & Charles*	1970	1·75
WEGG-PROSSER, CHARLES. The Police and the Law. *ISBN 0 85120 165 2.*	*Oyez*	1973	1·25

Note: Voluntary bodies concerned with criminal justice matters normally publish annual and other reports.

Printed in England for Her Majesty's Stationery Office by Henry Ling Ltd., Dorchester, Dorset.
Dd 223964/486 K24 2/75